"Bob Dylan is the master. If I'd like to be anyone, it's him. And he's a great writer, true to his music and done what he feels is the right thing to do for years and years and years. He's great. He's the one I look to."

Neil Young

"I think Bob Dylan is a genius and a poet. I admire his spirit and his music"

Paul McCartney

"Bob freed your mind the way Elvis freed your body. To this day, wherever great rock music is being made, there is the shadow of Bob Dylan."

Bruce Springsteen

"I've never bought a Dylan record. A singing poet? It just bores me to tears. If I had ten Dylans in the final of *American Idol*, we would not be getting 30 million viewers a week. I don't believe the Bob Dylans of this world would make *American Idol* a better show."

Simon Cowell

INSPIRATIONS SERIES

Series Editor: Rosemary Goring

An easy-to-read series of books
that introduce people of achievement
whose lives are inspirational.

Other titles in the series:

Robert Burns
Nelson Mandela
The Williams Sisters

Further titles to follow in 2011

Bob Dylan

nothing but mystery

Colin Waters

ARGYLL✠PUBLISHING

© Colin Waters 2010

Argyll Publishing
Glendaruel
Argyll PA22 3AE
Scotland
www.argyllpublishing.com

The author has asserted his moral rights.

**British Library Cataloguing-in-Publication Data.
A catalogue record for this book is available from the British Library.**

The publisher acknowledges subsidy from the Scottish Arts Council towards the publication of this volume.

ISBN 978 1 906134 51 8

Printing: JF Print Ltd, Somerset

To Anna,
Aurla and
Harris –
May you stay
forever young

Contents

Preface	7
1. Not the Boy Next Door (1941-59)	13
2. A Short History of Folk Music	20
3. On the Road (1959-61)	27
4. Civil Rights	33
5. The Apprentice (1961)	40
6. Cold War Blues	46
7. Hammond's Folly (1961-2)	52
8. Wind and Rain (1962)	58
9. Freewheeling (1962-3)	63
10. Love Again (1963)	66
11. Another Side (1963-5)	72
12. Going Electric (1965)	77
13. Goodbye to All That (1965)	82
14. Crash (1965-6)	87
15. Down in the Basement (1966-8)	93
16. Losing It (1968-74)	98
17. Rolling Thunder (1974-5)	103
18. Falling From Grace (1976-87)	109
19. World Gone Right (1987-2010)	114
Epilogue – Things Have Changed	119
Dylan – the Music: Where To Begin	124
Bibliography	127

Acknowledgements
The author would like to thank Graeme Blaikie
for access to his Dylan archives. Special thanks
to Clinton Heylin and Howard Sounes for their
books on Dylan over the years; the book couldn't
have been written without their pioneering work.
And of course, many thanks
to Bob Dylan himself.

Preface

THE BOOING began before Bob Dylan had even picked up his guitar. Followed on stage by his band, the Hawks, he ignored his audience. Dressed in a high-buttoned grey suit, with his bird's-nest hair unrulier than ever, Dylan was getting used to boos, and he knew how to handle them.

As the jeers and slow handclapping continued, he leaned into the mike and began to mumble nonsense just low enough to be heard but not understood. After a few moments, the noise in the hall quietened as the audience strained to hear what Dylan was saying. When finally the audience was silent, Dylan murmured, '. . . if you only just wouldn't clap so *hard*.' It got a laugh that was immediately crushed by the band piling in to play 'One Too Many Mornings'.

It was May 17th, 1966, and Bob Dylan was in Manchester playing the city's grand Free Trade Hall. The last time he played there, the reaction had been very different. A year earlier audiences who attended his first British tour had been respectful, and even reverent. But back then he was Bob Dylan, singer of protest songs. Now he was Bob Dylan, folk music traitor.

Folk music in the mid-sixties was largely enjoyed

by fans who were looking for an alternative to a mainstream they thought bland and compromised by commercialism. They hated the flavourless, non-political crooners their parents loved, the Doris Days and the Perry Comos. They also hated rock n' roll which they dismissed as noisy, incapable of the lyrical subtlety folk was capable of, and just as compromised by market forces as the older generation's easy listening.

Only folk music had the answer. For several years, the best argument on behalf of that view was Bob Dylan. Armed only with his acoustic guitar and his wit, Dylan first turned the folk music scene and then the American music industry on its head. Intelligent, compassionate, sometimes funny and always thought-provoking, his lyrics led many to reconsider what popular music could say and be. Songs such as 'Blowin' In The Wind' and 'The Times They Are A-Changin'' spoke eloquently about the era they were written in and yet had a timeless quality that would ensure they would still be listened to and argued over half a century later.

In July, 1965, however, at the Newport Folk festival, on Rhode Island, Dylan had decisively turned his back on his early supporters, or so they thought. He had rejected the folk scene that embraced him and brought him to prominence. And he did it in the worst way. At Newport, Dylan had played rock n' roll with an electric band.

Preface

He wanted to try something new, he said. His folk fans said he was selling out. Moreover, he seemed intent on flouting all that the audience held dear, especially the image they had of him. So they booed him at Newport. And they kept on booing. As Dylan toured America then on to Australia, Sweden, Ireland, Britain and France through late 1965 and into 1966, the boos got louder and the atmosphere at the gigs grew ever more fraught.

By May 1966, Dylan would be forgiven for feeling frazzled. He had to endure a constant round of interviews and press conferences in addition to travelling and performing. At the same time, he stayed up for days writing and playing, chasing down his latest tune. He was a whirl of activity, a man on fire.

In Glasgow, a waiter delivering room service suddenly turned abusive, called Dylan a traitor to folk music, and pulled a knife before being bundled out of the room. There were stage invasions. Fans didn't know whether to kiss him or kill him.

Dylan knew he was right, and so did his band. The rocked-up songs sounded titanic. Audience members likened the sound and the force it exerted upon them to a jet taking off. Although the boos kept coming, rock had rarely sounded so thrillingly (or loudly) alive. But between songs, Dylan stared into the audience, his face a mask.

The Manchester Free Trade Hall audience enjoyed the earlier, acoustic section of the show, a reminder of the first phase of Dylan's career, only for all hell to break loose when Dylan returned to the stage with the Hawks. People cried out 'Turn it down' and stuck their fingers in their ears. At the start of the electric show, a pretty, smiling girl walked to the front of the stage and handed Dylan a note. It read, 'Tell the band to go home'.

The mask cracked at the close of the Manchester show. Dylan snapped to life when, as the Hawks readied themselves to play their final number, a member of the audience cried: 'JUDAS!'

'I don't believe you,' Dylan drawled. His face deathly pale, Dylan looked away from the mike for a moment, only to return to cry, 'You're a liar'.

Dylan turned his back on the audience and, anger in his voice, commanded his band, 'Play f***ing loud'.

The Hawks launched into a monumental, murderous version of 'Like A Rolling Stone', his game-changing 1965 record. Dylan directed all of the song's anger at those who wanted to put him in a box, to make him a prisoner of the folk scene all his days. No. He wouldn't do it. There would be no compromising. No returning to the past.

This performance of 'Like A Rolling Stone' was bootlegged and spread amongst fans who heard in its thunderous groove the angry spirit of the age. Little wonder the Manchester Free Trade show has become one of the most written about moments in rock history.

Preface

What Dylan, his band, and the audience couldn't know was that these British shows would be Dylan's last tour for eight years. Nor would it be the last time Dylan was booed for launching a new direction on an unsuspecting audience.

* * *

Given his popularity, you would expect Bob Dylan's record sales to be in the Michael Jackson league. And over his 50-year-long career, he has sold 60 million records. Yet that figure is modest compared to Madonna or even Ozzy Osbourne, never mind big-leaguers like the Rolling Stones, Pink Floyd or David Bowie. The writer of over 600 songs, he's had surprisingly few hits, at least hits performed by himself. He's had more success as the writer of material covered by others than as a performer of his own songs.

And yet Dylan is the greatest popular songwriter of the latter half of the 20th century. His achievements cannot fail to impress. He reinvented lyric writing in popular song. He helped popularise folk music for a new generation in the 1960s. He was a leading light of the American civil rights movement, writing many of its most enduring anthems. He was a pioneer of folk-rock and country-rock. He arguably invented the promotional video. He is the ultimate example of the popular recording artist who follows his moods in the face of fierce opposition from fans and critics who want him to remain the way they like him.

Moreover, Dylan's life and music, particularly in their first phase, are perfect illustrations of American life in the first decades after World War II. The civil rights movement, the Cold War, the sixties' youthquake and loosening of morals – Dylan shaped and was shaped by these events.

Nor is his story over. Of his generation of musicians, he is the only one to continue releasing vital music. Since the turn of the twenty-first century, he has scored number one albums on both sides of the Atlantic. Important films and documentaries have been made about him. There has been a lot of Bob Dylan about. Yet the question remains – who is he?

Since his earliest days in New York as an unknown teenager hustling gigs in coffee houses, Dylan has cultivated a mystique. He hid his origins then, and even now, with so much more known about his life, there is a crucial *unknowability* about Dylan. He is full of contradictions. It's almost impossible to talk about Bob Dylan, only Bob *Dylans*. Through his career, fans have witnessed him change from Bob the folk singer to Bob the rocker, Bob the country crooner to Bob the preacher. It's this air of unpredictability that makes him fascinating.

1. Not the Boy Next Door

(1941-59)

BOB DYLAN was born Robert Allen Zimmerman in Duluth, USA, on May 25th, 1941. As a Jewish child, at birth he was given two names, Robert Zimmerman and his name in Hebrew, Shabtai Zisel ben Avraham. It's fitting he should be christened with two names, for throughout his performing career Dylan has had many identities.

Dylan's father Abe Zimmerman was the son of Jewish immigrants from the Russian (now Ukrainian) city of Odessa. The Zimmermans settled in Duluth in the state of Minnesota in 1905. Its wintry landscape possibly reminded the Zimmermans of the countryside they left behind. Like Odessa, Duluth was often very cold for long periods of the year.

Minnesota is part of the American Midwest and lies on the border with America's northern neighbour Canada. In the early part of the twentieth century, Duluth had a small but popular port; for a short time, it was the busiest port in the United States.

Dylan's mother, Beatrice Stone, was the child of a well-to-do Jewish family. They too were immigrants, from Lithuania. They had settled in Duluth's smaller, neighbouring town, Hibbing. Abe and Beatrice met in Duluth at a New Year's party. They married in 1934; he was 22 years old, she, 19. They were happy but it wasn't the greatest time to start a new life.

The American economy had fallen apart. The Wall Street Crash of October, 1929, led to the decade-long Great Depression, the greatest economic crisis of all time. The immediate effect of the Depression for the newly married Abe and Beatrice Zimmerman was to persuade them to delay having children until they could afford it. Abe held down a job at the petrochemical corporation Standard Oil, but he and his wife still felt they had to wait seven years before they could afford to have a child.

Dylan spent the first six years of his life in Duluth, before illness triggered a move. In 1946, Abe contracted polio, a disease that can cripple sufferers. The President of the United States when Dylan was born, Franklin D Roosevelt, was wheelchair-bound by polio he contracted at the age of 39. Until the 1950s, there were few effective remedies. Abe lost mobility and then he lost his job at Standard Oil. Abe, Beatrice and Robert had to relocate to Hibbing where they were helped by relatives during this difficult period.

Abe had to relearn how to walk. Once he was back on his feet, he went into business with his brothers, selling and repairing electrical goods. They began trading at just the right time. After their difficulties

Not the Boy Next Door (1941-59)

in the second half of the 1940s, the Zimmermans began to make a good living.

The 1950s dawned, and with it a new era began in America of prosperity and consumerism. World War II had been a time of great sacrifice for the country and people now wanted to enjoy the fruits of their struggles. The era was about maintaining stability after the upheavals of the 1930s and 1940s.

In character, the 1950s were outwardly conformist and calm. Young people of Dylan's generation who grew up in this period were called Baby Boomers. They were conceived and born in the years after World War II in great numbers. Baby Boomers would grow up to think of themselves as a special generation. In the 1960s, by virtue of their numbers, American Baby Boomers would attempt to remake America with mixed results. Dylan would play a major part in shaping the ambitions and ideals of his generation, sometimes reluctantly.

Hibbing was a young town, only founded in 1893. It was home to a large iron-ore mine where most of the locals worked, a typical small town, removed geographically from the sort of action that excites young minds. Like many young people, Dylan found his small hometown dull and he dreamt of leaving to explore the world outside.

One of the things that fired his imagination was music. The family acquired a piano, which is when Dylan first began to play music. His radio became important. It was his connection with the wider world. Musical heroes included the country and western singer Hank Williams. He also grew to love the blues, what was called 'race music' back then because blues performers – Muddy Waters, John Lee Hooker, Jimmy Reed – tended to be African American. It was almost impossible to buy 'race music' records in Hibbing, and there were hardly any African Americans living there either.

Elvis Presley was another early passion: 'When I heard Elvis's voice', Dylan said, 'I just knew that I wasn't going to work for anybody and nobody was gonna be my boss. Hearing him for the first time was like breaking out of jail.' It was true – apart from a brief stint as a bus boy in Fargo after graduating from high school, Dylan never had a regular job.

As a teenager Dylan bided his time. While he waited he kept playing the piano, and soon enough the guitar too; going to the cinema was his other passion. He was particularly taken, as so many of his generation were, with the movies stars James Dean (who died young in 1955, victim of a car crash) and French sex symbol Brigitte Bardot. 'Song To Brigit', a tribute to Bardot, is thought to be the first song Dylan wrote, sometime between 1956 and 1957.

At this point, Dylan was not interested in folk music, the music that made his name. His passion was for blues and early rock n' roll records. Although he was said to be somewhat shy and nervous as a

Not the Boy Next Door (1941-59)

teenager, Dylan formed his first band, the Jokers, an a cappella group, in 1956. He played concerts at his high school.

It was obvious to the young Robert Zimmerman that if you were going to perform, you needed a stage name. Most of the performers he liked had adopted names. This wasn't an attempt to hide his ethnicity, although prejudice against Jews lingered in America; it was to do with his understanding of what an artist is. Assuming an identity freed an artist, cut away the baggage of his past. It underlined the liberating effect of art: you could be anyone you want to be, you only have to dream it.

His first attempt at a stage name was the moody-sounding 'Elston Gunn'. He then tried 'Robert Allen', which he liked because it sounded like the name of a Scottish king. Then in the spring of 1958, he hit on a new alter ego: 'Bob Dylan'.

There are theories as to how Dylan arrived at the name. *Gunsmoke*, a popular Western TV show, had as its hero a cowboy character called Matt Dillon. Others say he took it from a Welsh poet he was reading at the time, Dylan Thomas. Thomas died comparatively young in 1953.

As he approached his late teens, Dylan became increasingly serious about making a living out of music. His parents, Abe in particular, a practical man, couldn't understand this. He might have been 'Bob Dylan' in his head but he was still plain Robert

Zimmerman to his parents, and if Abe had anything to do with it, he'd chase the nonsense out of his dreamer son's head.

Finally, after much wrangling, Dylan and his parents compromised. Dylan would go to college and only start a career in music once he had completed his education. Dylan agreed, though he possibly didn't take the deal as seriously as Abe did. Dylan might have been smart, but he was no scholar. Still, he respected his father and enrolled at the University of Minnesota.

The University of Minnesota was based in the Twin Cities of Minneapolis and St Paul, which were within the state of Minnesota. At the end of summer, 1959, Dylan moved to Minneapolis where he enrolled at the University in a liberal arts class with music as his major. The brief time he spent here is notable not for what he learned in class but off-campus.

Adjacent to the college campus there sat the bohemian neighbourhood of Dinkytown. Dylan was drawn to it. The rock n' roll he adored was not cool here. The music to namecheck was folk, just as the politics to practise were left-wing, and the book to read was Jack Kerouac's masterpiece *On The Road*.

On The Road was published in 1957 and has been described not so much as a novel as a cultural event. It concerns the adventures of Sal Paradise and Dean Moriarty as they travel by car from coast to coast. The spontaneity of the characters is matched by that of their slangy language. To teenagers in the 1950s, the novel presented an irresistible vision of freedom in a conformist era. Dylan said, 'It changed my life like it changed everyone else's.' *On The Road* spearheaded a new movement in American literature, called the Beats. Another Beat writer was Allen Ginsberg, poet, author of the long poem 'Howl', an openly gay man at a time when homosexuality was illegal, and a future friend of Bob Dylan.

Dylan fell head over heels for the whole Dinkytown scene and quickly swapped his electric guitar for an acoustic in order to play folk in clubs. What was this style of music that had so turned his head?

2. A Short History of Folk Music

FOLK MUSIC describes a style of music that dates back centuries, at least to the Elizabethan era. The term folk music is more modern, originating in the mid-nineteenth century. What it actually means is harder to say and has changed over the decades. What we can say is that, as the name implies, it's music that comes from folk, from people, that is, and that it's passed on orally from generation to generation. That's why folk music is also called traditional music. It was the music of peasants, of the rural poor, and its songs were held in common without individual authors.

By the 1920s, folk music was a mish-mash of elements, some of which would go on and develop into blues, country n' western, gospel, and early rock n' roll. The heart of folk music were the traditional songs, adaptations of Irish, Scottish and English folk ballads that had audiences in Shakespeare's time. These songs migrated from the British Isles to the Appalachian Mountains and Mississippi Delta, chang-

A Short History of Folk Music

ing a little on every step of the journey. Generally, folk was played on acoustic, unamplified instruments in keeping with its centuries-old roots: the fiddle, banjo, or guitar.

New York was the centre of the American recording industry in 1920. Companies on the make were hungry for novelty and for anything that would sell. Scouts were despatched to America's Deep South in search of new sounds. Here they found pockets of local musicians playing songs that had been in their family for decades. The scouts recorded these amateur musicians on a new invention, the tape recorder.

When the results were brought back to New York and pressed onto vinyl long-players, the records quickly found a market. New York was a city of immigrants, chiefly European, and they and their descendants were nostalgic for what they had left behind. Folk music reminded them of home. America was also the most industrialised country in the world in the 1920s, particularly its north, and this music from its south had a pre-machine age innocence that appealed.

Folk can cover any number of subjects but what appealed to many, including the young Bob Dylan, were the songs that dwelt on death and disaster. Many songs can be described as 'murder ballads' – tales of young women killed by jealous lovers or of infamous criminals of the day like Pretty Boy Floyd. It's not too much of a stretch to compare folk at its blackest lyrically with gangsta rap today.

When the demand for folk took off in the 1920s, and songwriters penned new folk songs to fill a gap in the market, they took their subjects straight from the newspapers. Folk sounded old as a mountain while its lyrics were as fresh as yesterday's headlines. Favourite subjects included the assassination of President McKinley in 1901, the sinking of the *Titanic* in 1912, and the breaking of the Mississippi levees in 1927.

The popularity of folk in the 1920s declined at the decade's end. In 1929, the American economy collapsed. After ten years of unprecedented growth, the economy shrank overnight when Wall Street traders realised as one that they had been paying too much money for the shares they owned. To recoup their profits, they sold their stocks and shares in a panic, reducing their value to almost nothing. Companies whose shares had been valued highly suddenly found their stock was worthless and had to close. Many Americans lost their jobs. Many more were left penniless when the cash they had invested disappeared with the companies they had bought shares in. Overnight many respectable Americans went from pillars of their community to the ranks of the unemployed. The numbers of the homeless swelled a hundredfold.

The Great Depression that followed the Crash

lasted almost a decade. It was a sad and desperate time for ordinary Americans. The homeless set up shantytowns on the fringes of major cities. Queues for soup kitchens stretched to the horizon. People were in terror of losing their jobs. There were many strikes and a great deal of industrial unrest which was often brutally put down by the civil authorities. They were terrified the Communism that had overthrown the Russian state in 1917 would get a foothold in America. Communism promised, in theory, to hand over control of the state and the factories to the workers, which naturally appealed to many who felt conned by the system.

One unforeseen consequence of the Depression was a revival of folk music. It won a new audience amongst the downtrodden for the way in which it described and encouraged their struggles. Folk singers in this period adapted traditional songs, penning new lyrics to old melodies. The most noted folk singer of the 1930s and the young Dylan's role model was Woody Guthrie.

Guthrie was born in a small town in Oklahoma in 1912. After a tragic early family life – his father went bankrupt, his seven-year-old sister died in a fire and his mother was committed to an insane asylum – Guthrie was left to fend for himself at the age of 14. He travelled round America, and by the time of the Depression, he was singing to the thousands of Okies heading towards California in search of work.

Okies were people from Oklahoma, usually agricultural workers. From 1930 to 1936, a drought combined with the effects of poor farming techniques turned Oklahoma's soil into dust that blew away, taking thousands of livelihoods with the wind. Those affected had no choice but to leave the state, with most of them heading for California. The labour conditions they encountered in California were brutal. Bosses treated the Okies like cattle. They had no one to stand up for them, other than folk singers.

Guthrie's best songs urge ordinary people to fight for social justice for all. His most famous song, 'This Land Is Your Land', asked Americans to recognise what they had in common and to reject laws that favoured the privileged.

The music of this period was hugely influential on the young Dylan. He would learn to make new songs by taking traditional melodies and adding his own up-to-date lyrics. He too would sing on behalf of the oppressed.

By the start of the 1960s, Guthrie was a victim of Huntingdon's Disease, an illness that affects co-ordination and gradually the mind. Guthrie's plight mirrored that of folk in the 1950s. Many of folk's leading lights in the 1930s and 1940s, musicians like Pete Seeger, held Communist and socialist beliefs, for which they were blacklisted by the authorities during a period of Cold War paranoia. Their music wasn't played on the radio and they weren't allowed to appear on television. Folk music was almost dead.

Then, in 1958 the Kingston Trio scored a Billboard number one with 'Tom Dooley', a murder ballad from 1866. The song's great success prompted a new folk boom with New York's bohemian quarter, Greenwich Village, as its hub. In fact, the Kingston Trio triggered two folk booms. One was a commercial version, a neat, preppy style played by clean-cut kids, which was urban, indeed, suburban.

The second boom grew out of the first, and it was for kids like Dylan who wanted to dig deeper, to hear the original gritty 1920s and 1930s records, in fact to return as close as they could to the source of folk. They tended to dismiss the more commercial version of folk. For them, the folk revival was about more than entertainment.

By the start of the 1960s, folk music had taken on a generational and political aspect. If you were an earnest, sensitive, and politically concerned young American in 1961, you more likely than not listened to folk music. From an early point in the revival, folk music and the civil rights movement became linked. Folk was seen as a hand-crafted, authentic expression of the American soul. It was idealistic, optimistic, and about community spirit as opposed to selfish individualism. It harked back to simpler times and was sometimes simplistic in the solutions it proposed as a cure for America's ills.

Like many his age in 1959, Dylan developed a mania for folk's new-old sound and was hungry to hear more and more. In the late 1950s it was difficult to hear a flow of fresh material, which led to some questionable behaviour on Dylan's part.

3. On the Road

(1959-61)

DYLAN had not long been a resident of Dinkytown when he grew obsessed with folk music. He was drawn to material that dramatised what rock critic Greil Marcus later called 'the old, weird America'. He liked narratives of sin and death, with powerful, emblematic characters and odd, quirky imagery – all hallmarks later on of his own lyrics. As he said himself:

> What folk music is, it's not Depression songs . . . The main body of it is just based on myth and the Bible and plague and famine and all kinds of things like that which are nothing but mystery and you can see it in all these songs. Roses growing right up out of people's hearts and naked cats in bed with spears growing right out of their backs and seven years of this and eight years of that and it's all really something that nobody can really touch.

He listened, when he could find someone who owned a copy, to the famed folklorist Alan Lomax's field recordings of traditional songs sung by prisoners, farmhands, and travelling bluesmen. He took on board a whole new set of musical influences that intoxicated him: Leadbelly (African American folk and blues singer covered by, amongst others, Johnny Cash, Led Zepplin, White Stripes, and Nirvana), Odetta (African American singer-songwriter, actress, and human rights activist, known as 'The Voice of the Civil Rights Movement'), Pete Seeger, and Woody Guthrie.

On first hearing Guthrie, Dylan later wrote, 'I was stunned – didn't know if I was stoned or straight. . . All these songs together one after another made my head spin. It made me want to gasp. It was like the land parted.'

Dylan began to dress like Guthrie, plainly in workshirt and overalls, and he imitated Guthrie's Okie drawl. He sang a wide selection of Guthrie's songs; he also paired Guthrie's tunes with lyrics of his own to create a 'new' song. He read *Bound For Glory*, Guthrie's autobiography, studying it until he had made Guthrie's way of talking his own.

Dylan attended parties held by friends where a guitar was passed round and people took turns singing for others. These parties were often raucous occasions with much alcohol consumed. Not coincidentally, Dylan stopped going to classes. The evening before his final exam of the year, he went to another party, got drunk, and sat his test while suffering a hangover. Somehow, he got a C grade.

Scruffy, shy, often awkward, Dylan was not to everyone's taste. One person he permanently alienated – and with good reason – was a fellow student whose record collection he borrowed without permission. When he left town for a fortnight – how's this for a sign of the times? – the student left his apartment unlocked. Dylan let himself into the apartment and took around 20 records.

When the student friend returned to find his collection gone, he guessed immediately that Dylan was the culprit. When confronted, Dylan denied the charge – until pinned against the wall. He returned the records. He had had no intention of selling them on. He took the records to hear the music, to expand the material in the growing number of songs he had memorised in order to perform them. It's worth remembering this took place at the start of the 1960s, a long time before CD reissues and downloads. In those days, it was often incredibly hard to get hold of or to even hear certain songs.

Whenever any folk artist played in the Twin Cities, Dylan was sure to be in the audience. He had the gift of being able to hear a song once and being able to play it back and recall the lyrics too.

As 1960 drew to a close, Dylan returned to Hibbing to tell his parents that he wanted to change their deal. He wanted to go to New York, simply had to go, and must leave as soon as possible. He had heard too much from visitors passing through Minneapolis about how great the music in New York's bohemian district Greenwich Village was to stay any longer. His parents didn't really understand his need but backed their 19-year-old son anyway. They'd help pay his way. He had a year to make a name for himself and if it wasn't working out, he was to return to Minnesota and resume his studies.

Dylan told his friends he was leaving for New York to become a star. Not many believed him. He had planned on spending Christmas with a girlfriend and her family but her parents didn't like him. Left alone in his flat on campus, Dylan upped and left without saying any formal goodbyes. 'When I arrived in Minneapolis, it had seemed like a big city or a big town. When I left it was like some rural outpost you see once from a passing train.'

Dylan stopped off along the way in Chicago for a few weeks before heading over to Madison, Wisconsin where he attended a Pete Seeger concert. In mid-January, Dylan hooked up with a University of Wisconsin student about to drive to New York with a friend and looking for a third person to share driving duties. Dylan annoyed the other two young men by singing Woody Guthrie songs all the way from Madison to New York.

On January 24th they arrived in the snow-bound streets of New York. New York in January 1961 was a cold city to visit, especially when you had no place to stay. A hard winter had settled in. You wouldn't guess it to look at Dylan that day what the future held for this pudgy kid, modestly dressed, only his

On the Road (1959-61)

bag and his guitar for company. A short time later, Dylan would commemorate his arrival in an early song, 'Talking New York', a time when the weather was cold enough to kill a man. The weather was to be merely the first test Dylan would face in New York.

He may not have had a place to stay but Dylan had a destination in mind. He started out for Greenwich Village, on the west side of lower Manhattan. The Village, as locals called it, had long been associated with the arts. Before the 1950s it had played a significant part in the history of the American theatre and the visual arts. In the 1950s, the Village was one of the birthplaces of the Beat scene which flowered in literature (*On The Road*) and music (jazz and blues). Artists and young people were attracted to the Village by its liberal attitude to sexual morality and personal grooming, and its openness to more experimental forms of the arts. They were called *Beatniks*. By the turn of the decade, the Village was the centre of the folk music revival, which was what interested Dylan.

That first cold January night in New York, Dylan made for *Café Wha?*, a folk club in the Village. As it was an open mike night, Dylan got on stage, dusted off his guitar and sang a couple of songs. After the show, the owner of *Café Wha?* asked the audience if anyone had a floor Dylan could sleep on that night. Dylan got his bed that night, and every night thereafter in New York. He had a certain charm that was useful when it came to securing a place to sleep or a meal or a slot in a club, or to borrowing money.

Playing music in coffee houses, as Dylan was set on doing, did not pay well. A folksinger earned his or her living passing a hat around the audience after his set. The Village folk scene had drawn to it many young people. Dylan would meet several friends and future stars as he moved from coffeehouse to coffeehouse, people like Carolyn Hester, Phil Ochs, Richie Havens, and Fred Neil.

Some of them came from working-class backgrounds, some from the middle class. Some were white, some black. What they had in common was youth, ambition, a love of folk and a belief it could play a part in re-shaping America. In particular, they were all involved to some degree in the civil rights movement. It was a struggle that Bob Dylan was to become closely associated with.

4. Civil Rights

THE CIVIL RIGHTS movement in America in the mid-twentieth century chiefly refers to the struggle African Americans undertook to claim the same legal rights enjoyed by the white majority population. The peak of the civil rights movement ran from 1955 to 1968, the period roughly in which Bob Dylan was involved.

The goals of the civil rights movement were twofold. To protect rights African Americans already had, such as the right to vote, but were largely denied through intimidation. And to campaign for new legislation which enshrined African Americans' rights to equal access to education and to equal rights in the work place and before the law with whites.

The civil rights movement's chief tactic in this period was non-violence inspired by the example of Mahatma Gandhi, whose supporters used it to win independence for India from the British Empire in the 1940s. The American civil rights movement pursued a policy of non-violence despite incredible provocation and assaults by their opponents. In the Deep South, their opponents included not just racist citizens. The authorities were often openly and proudly prejudiced and willing to go to violent extremes to stop the fight for civil rights.

The roots of this struggle go back to the beginning of America's history. The first English colony in North America in Virginia in 1607 was maintained by slave labour. Over the next two hundred years, black people were kidnapped from their homes in Africa, transported by boat across the Atlantic in squalid, murderous conditions, and forced to work on plantations and as domestic servants at the cost of their lives if they resisted.

By the nineteenth century, many countries around the world had outlawed slavery. Religious movements and debate convinced many it was morally wrong to enslave another human regardless of skin colour.

The argument was not decisively won in America and by the 1850s it was becoming a divisive issue in the country's politics. There was a split roughly along geographic and economic grounds. The South, which depended on slave labour to run its cotton, sugar and tobacco plantations, was pro-slave, whereas the North was slowly growing more anti-slavery.

In the 1860 Presidential election Abraham Lincoln had campaigned on the basis of restricting the enslavement of African Americans. Fearful that an outright banning of slavery across the whole of the United States was the inevitable next step when Lincoln won the Presidency, the slave states in the south broke away to form the Confederacy. Those states that did not break away formed the Union. The Union viewed the Confederacy's declaration of independence as an act of rebellion and treason, and so war began. A year after it began, Lincoln declared as a goal of war the abolishment of slavery across America. The American Civil War ran from 1861 to 1865, and has at times through Dylan's career been a source of fascination and inspiration.

When the Confederacy was defeated in 1865, slavery was abolished. But the War was an incomplete revolution. Although Lincoln outlawed slavery, in the Deep South there was little in the way of supervision of the new laws. African Americans were given the right to vote in 1865 but soon ways were found to stop them voting and to keep them virtual slaves, a situation that continued until Dylan's day. Tricksy legal measures were brought into play to keep the names of African Americans off voting registers, or more brutally, violence was used. The Ku Klux Klan, a white supremacist movement whose members hid their identity behind white hoods, waged campaigns of terror on black neighbourhoods with the aim of deterring African Americans from claiming their rights. 'Uppity' African Americans were often lynched by the Klan as a warning to their people.

Racism was apparent in other ways. There was racial segregation. Across the Deep South African Americans were expected to sit in a different part of a bus to white passengers on public transport, to drink from a different water fountain, and to eat in different areas of a diner, assuming they were allowed into the diner in the first place. They couldn't serve on juries and black education was underfunded to the point in some areas it was nonexistent.

Generally, African Americans were made to feel like second class citizens. Rules enforcing segregation were called 'Jim Crow' laws. Jim Crow was a character played by Thomas D. Rice, a white actor who 'blacked up' to mock African Americans as stupid and lazy. Somehow the term moved from the music hall to state and local laws covering the conduct of the races.

The civil rights movement had some early successes. In 1954, *Brown vs. Board of Education of Topeka* was a landmark ruling in US legal history. Here, the United States Supreme Court handed down a judgement ending the practice of educating blacks and whites separately. The state had argued that they pursued a principle of 'separate but equal' but as it was proven that the state had in fact starved black schools of money, the court dismissed their defence. It was the first step on the path to society-wide integration.

In 1955, Rosa Parks, an African American woman,

Civil Rights

was arrested after she refused to give up her bus seat for a white passenger in Montgomery, Alabama. Civil rights campaigners organised a boycott of Montgomery's bus service. As the transit system was used mostly by African Americans, the boycott financially crippled the service. By November 1956, a federal court ordered Montgomery's buses to desegregate. The campaign brought to national prominence the Southern baptist minister, Dr Martin Luther King Jnr, who led the boycott.

In 1957, in Little Rock, Arkansas, the state governor called in the National Guard to prevent nine African American students enrolling at a whites-only high school. The President, Dwight Eisenhower, counter-ordered the National Guard back to their barracks and ordered the 101st Airborne Division to protect the nine students. The students had to run a gauntlet of hate on the journey to and on their way around the school as local whites spat, swore and tried to injure them.

In 1960, black college students in Greensboro, North Carolina, sat down at the segregated counter in Woolworths, to protest the chain store's racist policy. It set off a wave of similar sit-ins across America. Often they were violently suppressed by the police or store security.

The following year, when Dylan arrived in New York, saw the start of what were called Freedom Rides. These were journeys made by young black and white civil rights campaigners on buses into segregated parts of America's south, testing another Supreme Court ruling forbidding segregation while travelling interstate. The buses were firebombed and activists were horribly beaten and thrown into jail.

One might have thought that as the child of white, relatively prosperous parents, Dylan would know little about the plight of African Americans in this period. The intensity of his pro-civil rights songs suggests otherwise, and for good reason. His family had experience of what happens when the state turns against its most vulnerable citizens.

In 1905, when the Zimmermans left Odessa, the Ukraine was a region within the larger state of Russia. During the nineteenth century, Odessa attracted a large number of Jews who settled and worked there. Russia in the early part of the twentieth century was often a harsh place for its Jewish citizens. The success the Jewish minority had achieved in business, politics and the arts attracted envy, which in turn led to anger and violence. Anti-Jewish riots, called *pogroms*, led to Jewish homes and businesses being attacked with the unspoken consent of the authorities. A particularly vicious pogrom in Odessa in 1905 persuaded the Zimmermans to emigrate.

Nearly sixty years later, when Bob Dylan became famous, he first became known as a singer of what were called 'protest songs'. 'Protest songs' were songs that had a liberal political slant and were associated with the civil rights movement. They protested wrongs. Dylan's songs in this period – 'Blowin' In The Wind', 'The Times They Are A-Changin' – were appeals for justice. So although not black, Dylan would not have been ignorant of the racism and persecution his grandparents suffered in Odessa, and some of this must have worked its way into his protest songs.

5. The Apprentice

(1961)

DYLAN had two ambitions when he arrived in New York. The first was to make a name for himself on the Village folk scene. The second was to meet Woody Guthrie. Dylan tried to visit Guthrie on his second day in New York. He travelled out to New Jersey to Greystone Park Hospital where Guthrie had been a patient since 1956 because of his illness, Huntingdon's Disease. He was unsuccessful on that occasion.

On January 29th, however, he managed to meet his hero after charming his way into the household of married friends of Guthrie who lived in New Jersey. Because of the proximity of their home to Greystone, they took Guthrie home every weekend to see other friends and his family.

Dylan wasn't the first young man to pay homage. Dylan's future friend, the singer Ramblin' Jack Elliott, for example, was a regular guest. Although he could no longer play or even communicate much, Guthrie

The Apprentice (1961)

loved to hear that the old songs had been passed on to the next generation. Dylan began to visit on a weekly basis though whether Guthrie recognised him from week to week is doubtful: Huntingdon's had affected Guthrie's mind badly by 1961.

So, within one week of arriving in New York, Bob Dylan had fulfilled his two ambitions: he had played coffee houses in Greenwich Village and he had met and sung for his hero, Woody Guthrie. Young Dylan, it is clear, was an unusually confident and ambitious teenager.

Soon, Dylan began to be noticed by Village natives. Who was he, this kid? Where had he come from? Where'd he get that Okie accent? Just who was Bob Dylan? For the time being, he wasn't telling.

When Dylan's new friends asked him about his background, he deflected inquiries with jokes or a tall tale. There was, a few guessed, something he didn't want to discuss, but whether it was a matter worth hiding or merely embarrassment about his origins, they didn't know yet.

To some, Dylan said he had been a carnival hand and blues singer in Gallup, New Mexico. He also claimed to have raced motorcycles and worked as a farmhand. As his name became better known and his reputation grew, Dylan's stories about his past seemed to tie in with the sort of songs he was singing.

Some people were sceptical, however, not least

because he changed his story on occasion. While drunk, Dylan told the folk singer Dave Van Ronk that he was in fact descended from Native Americans: 'I remember he solemnly gave us a demonstration of Indian sign language, which he was obviously making up as he went along.'

Folk songs often tell a shaggy dog story, and so Dylan may have felt emboldened by his chosen field of song to embellish the bare details of his background. He no doubt felt that his middle-class origins undermined the gritty songs about the downtrodden that he was singing at that time. If so, by pretending to be something he wasn't, he was playing a dangerous game.

For folk music was as ferociously fixated on authenticity, on 'keeping it real', as decades later the gangsta rap scene would be – minus the drive-by shootings of course. The thinking on the folk scene went: the older and more obscure the song, the better. Folksingers were not so much encouraged to write new material as to collect and pass on the songs of the past. Years later Dylan recalled, 'I was only doing a few of my songs back then. . . You'd just try to sneak them in. The first bunch of songs I wrote, I never would say I wrote them.'

Dylan already had an impressive number of folk songs memorised, and was ready to take more on board. Indeed, he irritated other singers by copying their arrangements of traditional songs. After meeting

The Apprentice (1961)

at Woody Guthrie's hospital bed, Dylan followed around Ramblin' Jack Elliott to an extent that finally exhausted the older man's patience. Dylan copied Elliott's performing style, even the way he held his guitar. At this stage, Dylan was taking and adapting the best of the qualities he saw in his fellow performers with a speed and skill that undermines the early public perception of Dylan as a folk singer with a gift for words who just happened to be in the right place at the right time. Dylan had ambition alright, more than his peers realised at the time.

This first year in New York was Dylan's apprentice period, the time he spent readying himself to write the songs that made his name, a time of gathering experience and knowledge. Many days he could be found at the Village's Folklore Centre, educating himself about the history of these 'handed-down' songs. Here, he found what he couldn't in mainstream culture.

He began a thorough programme of self-education. In his first year in New York, he read intensely and widely. He read Russian and English Romantic poets, ancient Greek historians, German military strategists, and a biography of Civil War general Robert E. Lee.

The American Civil War is a recurring subject of interest for Dylan. In the reading rooms of the New York Public Library, he scanned newspapers dating from 1855 to 1865 on microfiche. The period covers the American Civil War; the war inspired many folk songs which were still being sung in the Village, some by Dylan himself. Within the year he'd write his own song about the era, 'John Brown', a bitter tale of a maimed soldier returning to his mother. Dylan was greatly attracted by the power of myth; moreover, he was attracted by the power music had to shine a new light on something shabby and troublesome like a murder or a flood or a failed harvest, to turn it into something mythic.

It's interesting that Dylan should initially look not to his own times but into the past. After all, the newspapers of his day were full of articles ready to be transformed into songs, and before long Dylan would do just that. But he had his eyes on a longer game, and if the future fans of his protest songs knew what was on his mind, they'd have been surprised: 'The madly complicated modern world was something I took little interest in. It had no relevancy, no weight.'

It's an amazing thing, to hear the soon-to-be-hailed 'voice of a generation' admit that the modern world 'had no relevancy' to him. Bear in mind, four days prior to Dylan's arrival in New York, John Fitzgerald Kennedy had been inaugurated as the 35th President of the United States of America. At the age of 43, he was the youngest President elected to office, and his youth seemed to confirm the dawn of a new, more idealistic era.

The Apprentice (1961)

On the other side of the Atlantic, another set of key contributors to the decade's 'youthquake', the Beatles, played their first gigs at the Cavern Club in Liverpool. Something was happening.

If Dylan was moved by anything in the early 1960s, however, it wasn't so much optimism as dread. And these were dread-filled days. America faced serious challenges. A period of international tension, the Cold War was in full swing, and Dylan, like everyone else on the planet, had to live with the potentially cataclysmic potential consequences of the nuclear bomb. His way of coping was writing songs about it.

6. Cold War Blues

THE COLD WAR was the diplomatic and military stand-off between the USA and the Communist USSR that lasted from the end of World War II to the collapse of the USSR in 1991. After the defeat of Nazi Germany, the USA and Russia, or as it called itself the USSR, were the two most powerful countries in the world. They were dubbed superpowers. During World War II they had been allies but now their common Nazi enemy had been defeated they became rivals struggling to win influence in the same regions of the world.

Two powerful groups of countries aligned around the superpowers. The West, centred on the USA, gathered together the Western democracies which broadly supported a form of capitalism. After World War II, America funded the reconstruction of Western Europe because they were concerned that if left unaided, the people of those countries in their bitterness might go over to supporting the Communists. The countries who were aided went on to sign a treaty in 1949 promising to come to each other's aid in the event of an attack. The treaty formed the North Atlantic Treaty Organisation, or NATO for short.

The Eastern bloc comprised the USSR and the European countries (Poland, Czechoslovakia, Hungary, Romania, Bulgaria, East Germany) it had freed from the Nazis only then to install puppet governments. Those who lived within the Russian sphere of influence were expected to obey the new regime without question. Nor were they allowed to leave for the West. In 1946, wartime Prime Minister Winston Churchill made a speech in America in which he described this European split as 'an iron curtain'. The phrase stuck. In 1955, these 'iron curtain' countries signed a treaty which established the Warsaw Pact which was intended to be the Communist version of NATO.

Now two heavily armed camps sat facing each other. If they didn't attack each other, it was because both sides had nuclear weapons. America developed its nuclear bomb during World War II. The nuclear devices that were dropped by the Americans on Nagasaki and Hiroshima in 1945 are credited with bringing World War II to a sudden end. The damage the bombs inflicted on Japan was so horrific the Japanese government quickly sued for peace.

By 1949, the USSR had its own nuclear bombs, beginning an arms race between the superpowers. Both countries spent a lot of money building more bombs and developing deadlier technology, to the extent neither country dared to attack the other. Both sides had enough nuclear weapons to destroy themselves and the world many times over. The scenario preventing an all-out nuclear showdown was called Mutually Assured Destruction, or MAD.

The situation might have brought peace to the world but no one was quite sure how long it could last. Many ordinary people felt their lives put under an intolerable strain by the international situation. With the images of Hiroshima and Nagasaki fresh in their minds, they formed peace movements campaigning for nuclear disarmament. Dylan's contribution was to write songs that capture the era's aura of nuclear dread.

Although described as a Cold War, there were flashpoints that threatened to turn hot. Following World War Two, Germany was split into two, West and East. Within the Eastern territory controlled by Russia, the German capital, Berlin was divided again into an eastern portion controlled by the USSR and the western half jointly supervised by America, Britain and France. In 1948, the USSR blocked road and rail routes into West Berlin in a bid to take complete control of the city. To thwart the blockade, America began to fly supplies into Berlin, daring the Russians to shoot down one of their planes. Such an incident would have led to World War III. It didn't happen and after almost a year, the Russians admitted defeat and lifted the blockade. In 1961, however, to prevent further East Berliners escaping to the Western sector, Soviet authorities built a city-wide wall along the divide in Berlin.

Instead of open warfare, the superpowers supplied weaponry and know-how to sympathisers, be they the government or guerrillas, in countries outside their immediate spheres of influence such as Guatemala, Persia, and the Philippines. Many nationalist movements in countries attempting to gain the freedom to run their own affairs from colonial masters such as the British and the French Empire were allied with local Communist parties. Fearing rising Communist influence, America intervened in these countries' domestic affairs. The Americans, who publicly preached the virtues of liberty and condemned the Russians for crushing freedom, were happy to see dictators installed as long as they weren't Communist dictators. This created a certain cynicism back in America about the motives of their own country's government that would grow over the decade, a doubt that Dylan initially appeared to share with many people of his age.

One place the Americans intervened was Vietnam, where a Communist-backed nationalist movement was attempting to free the country from French colonial rule. Eventually the French left, but the Americans were not content to see Vietnam fall to the Communists. The government feared a 'domino effect'. If they let one country go, the whole region might fall to Communism state by state. Over a decade, America scaled up its presence in Vietnam until they were involved in a full-on war with the North Vietnamese guerrilla army.

As the killing of Vietnamese and young Americans drafted to fight the war increased, many of Dylan's generation asked themselves whether the war was worth it and began to protest against it. Dylan songs such as 'Masters Of War' and 'With God On Their Side' were bitterly anti-war.

The Cold War also took the form of a technological competition dubbed the Space Race. At first the Soviets outpaced the Americans. In 1957, they launched the first artificial satellite to orbit the earth, *Sputnik*. It would be another year before the Americans launched their own satellite. The Russians' lead caused great concern in America and a political crisis. The Americans were determined not to be beaten by the Russians again. Both countries began to send animals into space as a precursor to sending a man. Then, in 1961, the Russian cosmonaut Yuri Gagarin became the first man in space. With the Russians beginning to look predominant in the field of space exploration, the Americans made it a priority to reach the moon first, which they did in 1969.

The public was excited by the race to the moon, though more sceptical voices asked whether humans weren't better off sorting out their problems on earth before heading off to other planets and at great expense too.

With the civil rights movement challenging America from within, and the Cold War challenging from without, America experienced unusually turbulent times in the 1960s. And there was Dylan in New York, channelling the dread and fear and yet also the optimism many his age felt about changing the world. Out of this powerful mix of emotions he would fashion his era-defining songs. He didn't know it as 1961 continued nor did anyone else but he was on the verge of his first major breakthrough.

7. Hammond's Folly

(1961-2)

DYLAN'S first self-penned numbers were not the dense, serious songs he would soon become associated with. Quite the opposite. Looking to lighten the mood in a set mostly made up of covers of anti-war songs and murder ballads, Dylan penned a number of humorous songs. He based them on the 'talkin' blues' model of songs Woody Guthrie excelled at: long, strummed songs over which the singer elaborates ever sillier turns of events.

Dylan wrote several in his first year or so in New York; they had the virtue of being easy to play and showcased his way with words. One example plucked from the headlines was 'Talking Bear Mountain Picnic Massacre Blues', a fantastical exaggeration of a story he read about an oversold boat trip that turned into a brawl. In Dylan's version, the ship sinks amidst a riot.

Slowly but surely, Dylan was becoming known in the Village. He was getting closer to writing his first major songs. But something was missing, some vital piece of experience that would broaden his world view and emotional range. By summer, he found it, when he fell in love with the woman who was to be his first major inspiration.

Hammond's Folly (1961-2)

Suze Rotolo was seventeen when Dylan met her in the summer of 1961. They met at a live broadcast Dylan was taking part in. Instantly, he was smitten. It was love and it changed Dylan and his songwriting.

Suze (pronounced 'Suzie') and her sister Carla were born and bred in Queens, New York, the children of Italian-American parents involved in union activism and left-wing politics. Both sisters shared their parents' political sympathies. Carla worked as a secretary to the musicologist Alan Lomax. Dylan had listened to and been inspired by Lomax's famous field recordings while still living in Dinkytown. Thanks to Carla's association with Lomax the Rotolo sisters were present at the radio show where they met Dylan for the first time. Dylan was to spend many days at Carla's flat listening to her substantial collection of folk and blues records. He heard there many of the songs he chose to cover on his first album.

Before long, Suze and Dylan were dating, and her influence on him was soon felt. She painted, sparking Dylan's interest in art. Suze brought to Dylan's attention the French symbolist poet Arthur Rimbaud (who wrote all his poetry before he was 20). He was deeply struck by something Rimbaud wrote: '*Je est un autre*' or 'I is someone else'.

'When I read those words,' he wrote, 'the bells went off. It made perfect sense.'

Unbeknownst to his friends in New York, before

arriving in town Dylan had already completed one self-reinvention. He had changed from the son of a Midwestern shopkeeper to a travelling Okie in the style of Woody Guthrie. As the years and his career progressed, his music and his stage persona would change again and again, some of these changes proving bewildering to his fan base. Not to Dylan though, who, if his response to Rimbaud shows anything, grasped at an early point in his career that his musical identity was not fixed for all time and could remain creatively unstable for many years to come.

Suze's influence was also political. She was involved in the civil rights movement, and through her, Dylan became involved too. His song lyrics became political, moving away from comic stories.

It took him about six months, until the start of 1962, for Dylan to process the effect Suze had had on him, and when he did he wrote 'The Death Of Emmett Till'. It was his first 'protest song'. It concerned a true story. Emmett Till was a 14-year-old African American who was lynched for whistling at a white woman in 1955 in Mississippi. Two white defendants accused of Till's murder were acquitted by a white jury. The acquittal was one of the factors that led to the formation of the American Civil Rights Movement.

Writing 'The Death Of Emmett Till' freed up something inside Dylan. New songs began to pour from his guitar.

Hammond's Folly (1961-2)

It was a good time for Dylan. As 1961 drew to a close, he was signed to Columbia, the largest record company in America at the time. The signing was a surprise to Dylan. The larger record companies did not normally trouble themselves to release folk records. There wasn't thought to be any money in it. In fact, the major record companies were dismissive of folk music.

Dylan had already approached the small, folk record label, Folkways, but it hadn't been interested. To make money and gain experience, Dylan played harmonica on a record made by his friend the folk singer Carolyn Hester when she signed to Columbia. A&R executive John Hammond was signing up folk-revival acts and was responsible for Hester's place on the Columbia roster. Hammond was present at the rehearsal session at Hester's flat where Dylan played harmonica. He must have heard something he liked because he asked Dylan to audition for him. After the audition, Hammond signed Dylan, who joined Columbia at the end of September 1961. The world might be going to perdition but things were coming together for Bob Dylan.

At the same time Dylan signed his record contract, he began a fortnight's residency at the Village club *Gerde's Folk City* and was attracting the first positive press coverage of his career. This in turn brought him to the attention of Albert Grossman, a promoter who wanted to manage Dylan. Grossman's reputation as a ruthless operator was at odds with the folk scene's left-wing bias and obsession with authenticity as opposed to show business. Nevertheless within a short period, Grossman had persuaded Dylan to let him be his manager.

Hammond moved fast and by November, he and Dylan began recording what would become his first album, Dylan accompanying himself on guitar and harmonica. The album was recorded in three short sessions in the last week of November. Dylan's lack of studio experience showed.

'Bobby popped every *p*, hissed every *s*, and habitually wandered off mike. Even more frustrating, he refused to learn from his mistakes,' Hammond said. Until that point in his career, he had 'never worked with anyone so undisciplined before'.

Dylan refused to record more than one take of a song, valuing freshness over perfection, a trait that continues to this day, sometimes to a song's disadvantage. He also annoyed Village associates by claiming credit as the arranger of the traditional songs he covered on that record; the arrangement, for example, Dylan performed of 'House Of The Rising Sun' was in fact worked up by Dave Van Ronk.

Perhaps his friends would have been more annoyed if the album had sold in greater numbers, but it failed to chart when it was released in March 1962, selling somewhere between a measly 2,500 and 5,000 copies. Dylan was dubbed 'Hammond's folly' and there was some muttering at Columbia about

Hammond's Folly (1961-2)

dropping Dylan (he or any act today who sold so poorly would most certainly be ditched). But the album was cheap to record and folk albums in those days sold modestly anyway. He would be allowed to record at least one more album.

What the execs didn't know was that Dylan was on the verge of writing one of the most famous songs of the second half of the twentieth century.

8. Wind and Rain

(1962)

DYLAN claimed to have written the lyrics to 'Blowin' In the Wind' in ten minutes, though, like many of his accounts of the creation of his songs, one should be cautious. He premiered the song at *Gerde's Folk City* in April, 1962, where it immediately got a good response from customers.

Hardened folkies (as folk fans were called) weren't as impressed. They recognised the melody as having been taken from the traditional anti-slavery song 'No More Auction Block'. Yet a year later 'Blowin' In The Wind' had become a civil rights anthem.

The lyrics, which are yearning rather than straightforwardly political, explain the song's appeal. Dylan asks a number of questions without obvious answers. Each inquiry is cumulative, contributing to the song's great unasked question: when will man stop oppressing his brother?

At the chorus, Dylan suggests an answer might or might not be found in the song's title – blowing in the wind.

Does that mean the answer is obvious or as hard

Wind and Rain (1962)

to grasp as the wind itself? Is the song a lament or a call to arms? Early fans of the song were in little doubt that the song was meant to raise awareness of specific current political issues. And for the first time, Dylan reached a black audience for whom the lyrics had great significance in the civil rights era.

But looked at again, the song could be understood in a number of ways. You'll notice the song actually contains no specific or contemporaneous references at all. No actual names, nothing about the rights of African Americans. Dylan arranges a sequence of images framed as questions; it's up to the listener how he or she wants to interpret them.

'Blowin' In The Wind' is the rock upon which Dylan built his career. Eventually it would be covered by hundreds of musicians, and has been translated into a number of languages, from Italian and German to Romanian and Bengali. No one has ever done a better version than Dylan's own mournful take.

During 1962, Dylan's relationship with Suze became strained. They were arguing, and the cracks in their relationship were not helped by the realisation she'd be leaving New York soon. She had enrolled at the University of Perugia and was departing for Italy with her mother at the start of June. Dylan was broken-hearted.

His pain inspired a new direction in his songwriting. He began to write songs that moved between the ache the separation caused him and something more stand-offish.

One song illustrates the change in his songwriting. 'Don't Think Twice, It's All Right' is a perfect illustration of the mixed feelings one might feel at the end of a troubled relationship. In the liner notes to *The Freewheelin' Bob Dylan*, the album 'It's All Right' appeared on, Dylan says the track isn't a love song. 'It's a statement that maybe you can say to make yourself feel better.' During the course of the song Dylan sounds casual, heart-broken, noble, mean, accusatory, nostalgic – all the emotions that tumble out at the close of a love affair.

It was with protest songs, however, that Dylan was to achieve prominence. And in the summer of 1962, with Suze in Italy, Dylan wrote arguably the most apocalyptic song of his career, 'A Hard Rain's A-Gonna Fall'.

It was a frightening time. In October, the world held its breath during what became known as the Cuban Missile Crisis.

In 1959, freedom fighters led by Fidel Castro and Che Guevara had overthrown Cuba's corrupt and cruel government. The previous regime had been pro-American, however, and a lot of businesses in the States which had invested in Cuba did not welcome this change in leadership because they lost their money. They made their views plain to the American government which began to grow hostile towards

Wind and Rain (1962)

Castro. For his part, Castro refused to hold democratic elections. Fearing America, Cuba's government turned Communist and sought support from the USSR.

Geographically, Cuba sat on America's doorstep, just off the coast of Florida. After the Cuban government turned Communist, America made life difficult for the island, imposing trading sanctions on the Cubans. Russia helped Cuba with money and goods, and in return the Russians had a favour to ask. It wanted to secretly install missile bases on the island in retaliation for the US building its own missile bases in Turkey on its border with Russia. America could not tolerate offensive missiles pointed in its direction only 90 miles from its Florida coast. So began the showdown.

America sent its navy to intercept Russian warships sailing to Cuba with missiles. A wrong move on either side could lead to a nuclear war. The world waited and wondered. The crisis was resolved when the Russians backed off in return for President Kennedy's secretly-made assurance he'd remove US missile bases from Turkey.

Earlier that year, in the summer, Dylan had written 'Hard Rain'. He debuted it in September at a concert held at New York's Carnegie Hall. Within a month, the Cuban Missile Crisis took place. Initial publicity for the song suggested it was written during the 13 days over which the Crisis took place. It wasn't, but the lyrics and world events were such a match, they became powerfully fixed together in people's minds.

The power of the song is such that it long ago outgrew the circumstances that gave birth to it. The Cold War ended in 1991, but in an era fearful of ecological disaster, the nightmare visions of 'Hard Rain' remain regrettably relevant.

Unlike 'Blowin' In The Wind', 'Hard Rain' was an immediate hit with other folkies, and was soon being covered all over the Village. Later, Dylan told an interviewer, '[When] I wrote ['Hard Rain'] – every line in that is really another song. . . I wrote that when I didn't know how many other songs I could write. . . I wanted to get the most down I knew about into one song as I possibly could. . . It's not atomic rain, it's just a hard rain. It's not the fall-out rain. It isn't that at all. I just mean some sort of end that's just gotta happen.'

Dylan's career was just starting however. His next move was to take his music abroad for the first time. London was calling.

9. Freewheeling

(1962-3)

BY DECEMBER, Dylan had recorded much of the material he would include on his second album. He broke off recording to travel to London where he had agreed to play several songs in a play broadcast on the BBC, *Madhouse On Castle Street*. While there, Dylan made contact with the local folk scene. He received a snotty reception in folk clubs when he sang; if anything, British traditionalists were even more conservative than their American counterparts. 'He went down like a lead balloon,' remembered one. 'He did a bad imitation of Woody Guthrie.'

Dylan made friends with younger folk artists like Martin Carthy. Carthy recalled, 'He had fabulous presence and a great sense of comedy.' The winter of 1962-3 was unusually cold and long, the coldest in fact since British records began. One day, to keep warm, Carthy and Dylan chopped up a piano for firewood with a samurai sword in his flat in Belsize Park. More significantly, Carthy introduced Dylan to many folk songs he had not heard, including 'Scarborough Fair'.

In January 1963, Dylan left London for Italy, hoping to meet Suze. Unbeknownst to him, she had left Perugia for New York, and Dylan found himself alone in Italy. Returning to London before flying back to New York, Dylan played Carthy a song he wrote in Italy, the aching 'Girl From the North Country'. The melody, Carthy noted, was taken from 'Scarborough Fair'. The sentiment was equally clear if you knew Dylan; he was missing Suze mightily.

Back in New York, Dylan and Suze reconciled. In the frosty early months of the year, they had their photo taken at the corner of Jones Street and West 4th Street for the cover of Dylan's forthcoming *Freewheelin'* album. It's one of the most famous album covers of the Sixties. The lovers hold each other tightly as they take a tentative stroll down the icy road; it seemed to echo the hopeful feelings of a new generation about to take their own first steps into the world.

Freewheelin' was released on May 27th. It was the album that would make Dylan's name internationally. Future friends and collaborators, George Harrison and John Lennon (from the Beatles) and the singer Van Morrison admitted to being blown away when they first heard it. The rawness of the melodies coupled with the song's lyrical sophistication was irresistible. Harrison in particular was struck by 'some vital energy, a voice crying out somewhere, toiling in the darkness'.

Freewheeling (1962-3)

He was right to feel that way. *Freewheelin'* is a strong, varied album, ranging in style and subject from love to comedy to civil rights.

In the same month, Dylan was invited to perform on *The Ed Sullivan Show*, a variety show watched by millions of Americans. In February of the following year, the Beatles would make their live American television debut watched by 73 million viewers, a record at the time.

Dylan chose to perform 'Talkin' John Birch Paranoid Blues', a spoof of Communist paranoia. The John Birch Society was a right-wing group who saw Communist influence everywhere. In the song, Dylan suggests the Society may have had opinions in common with Hitler and the Nazis.

Sullivan's producers were concerned the lyrics were libellous and asked him to play another song. By way of contrast, in 1967, when the Rolling Stones were asked to tone down the lyrics of 'Let's Spend The Night Together', the self-styled rebels complied. Dylan, however, refused – and walked off the set. He lost the chance to play to the biggest audience of his career, but his reputation as the uncompromising voice of youth was greater than ever now. He was growing into his role as the king of the folk scene. But every king needs a queen.

10. Love Again

(1963)

ONE PERFORMER who was quick to realise Dylan's talent was Joan Baez. When they met, Baez was arguably the biggest name on the folk scene. She was certainly a great deal better known than Dylan. She was darkly pretty and blessed with a voice that could penetrate armour. As 1963 dawned, she began to slip more and more Dylan songs into her live shows and to promote him as a great and upcoming talent.

In May, Dylan played the Monterey Folk Festival, with Baez watching from the side of the stage. During a performance of 'With God On Our Side', Baez sang with Dylan. Baez's and Dylan's voice didn't actually gel terribly well: her wineglass-shattering vibrato and his nasal drone were not the greatest of fits. The audience loved it though. After the Festival, Dylan travelled with Baez to her home in Carmel, and although he was living with Suze in an apartment on 4th Street, it was here they began a relationship.

Born in New York in 1941 with a Scots-Mexican

Love Again (1963)

ancestry, Baez learned to play the ukulele at an early age. When she was eight she was taken to a Pete Seeger concert. Seeger's performance inspired in Baez an enduring love of folk, and by the time she was in her teens, she was playing coffee shops in Boston, where her family had moved to. She caught the ear of an established folk singer who invited her to play unbilled with him at the 1959 Newport Folk Festival, the highlight of the folk music calendar. The performance made her a star. A year later she recorded her first album, *Joan Baez*. She was heavily involved with the civil rights movement, a friend of Martin Luther King Jnr, and she had a hit with the movement's anthem, 'We Shall Overcome'.

No doubt she approved when Dylan travelled to a rally in Greenland, Mississippi in July 1963 to perform at a civil rights rally. Here he played 'Only A Pawn In Their Game', a new song about the murder of local civil rights campaigner Medgar Evers. Evers was assassinated by white supremacist Byron De La Beckwith, the case causing a national uproar. Two juries failed to reach a verdict on whether De La Beckwith killed Evers. It took until 1994 before De La Beckwith was found guilty of Evers' murder.

The killing also inspired songs by several other songwriters. In Mississippi Dylan performed before a mainly African American audience (a moment captured on the Dylan tour film *Dont Look Back*). The new song demonstrated Dylan's ever-deepening craft; whereas other folkies who wrote on the same subject merely attacked the murderer, Dylan's song was about the larger social forces that profit from racism.

During the same month, Dylan's image as a musician for troubled times was further fixed when a cover version of 'Blowin' In The Wind' by the folk-pop trio Peter, Paul and Mary (who were one of Dylan's manager Albert Grossman's acts) reached number two on the US Hot 100 chart. It also became an international hit, selling over a million copies. Peter, Paul and Mary's next single, Dylan's 'Don't Think Twice, It's All Right', climbed to number nine, starting off a rush of Dylan covers in the charts. It's been a feature of Dylan's career that other recording artists have had more chart success with his songs than he has.

Another turning point was the Newport Folk Festival, held at the end of July. At the close of the Festival Dylan joined a number of other folk acts, including Peter, Paul and Mary and Joan Baez, to sing 'We Shall Overcome' and 'Blowin' In The Wind', a moment that confirmed his status as one of the most important singer-songwriters of the day. Newport was a triumph for Dylan.

And yet, already Dylan was chafing at being described as a protest singer. He felt it was limiting. He had no desire to sing only protest songs forever. He had wider ambitions. Dylan may have disliked being labelled but he was also canny, and so for the time being, he was content to ride the protest train –

at least until he no longer needed it. It paid off. *Freewheelin'* was selling 10,000 copies a week in this period.

The affair with Baez wasn't public knowledge yet, but Suze knew, and she moved out of their apartment in August. Dylan joined Baez's tour as a support act, also coming on during her set to sing a few numbers together. Quickly, they became the 1960s equivalent of an It couple.

Baez began to notice that although Dylan was writing songs that spoke deeply to many young people involved in the civil rights movement, he rarely attended rallies or went on demos. He was bored by discussions of politics. When pushed on this point, Dylan shocked Baez by claiming he only wrote his anti-war song 'Masters Of War' to make money. The intensity of its lyrics and its performance on *Freewheelin'* are an eloquent dismissal of its author's claim – he was no doubt teasing the occasionally humourless Baez – but it's true, whatever Dylan had in mind with regards to his songwriting, activism was not his goal.

Art and politics, no matter how worthy the cause, rarely work well together. The demands of one tend to cancel out those of the other, or else make a mess of both. In this contest, Dylan was only ever interested in making great art. He'd found a way to make songs out of topical material, but his interest in it was as just that, as material. When he lost interest (which was to happen soon), he'd look for his material elsewhere. Baez, on the other hand, campaigns on a number of issues to this day. And that is the difference between the pair. It wasn't so clear to Baez back then. But it was to Dylan.

Nevertheless, on August 28th, 1963, Dylan and Baez featured on the same bill as Martin Luther King Jnr at the March on Washington for Jobs and Freedom. It was here before the Lincoln Memorial that King gave his famous 'I have a dream' speech, and where Dylan played 'Only A Pawn In Their Game'. 300,000 people marched that day, with 80 percent of the protesters African American. The March is credited in part with helping to get passed in Congress the Civil Rights Act (1964), which outlawed racial segregation, and the National Voting Rights Act (1965), which outlawed discriminatory voting practices that prevent African Americans voting.

Dylan was growing ever more famous. It was inevitable journalists would begin to dig deeper into his background. Was he really a carnival hand from New Mexico? A rail-riding hobo made good? In October, he told *Newsweek*, the American weekly news magazine, that 'I don't know my parents. They don't know me. I've lost contact with them for years'. Dylan didn't know it but he was walking on thin ice. *Newsweek* reporters were onto him. And on November 4th, *Newsweek* shared what it had discovered with its readers:

Love Again (1963)

He shrouds his past in contradictions, but he is the elder son of a Hibbing, Minnesota, appliance dealer named Abe Zimmerman; and, as Bobby Zimmerman, he attended Hibbing High School, then briefly the University of Minnesota.

Far from being a half-starved son of the dustbowl who pulled himself up by his boot- (and guitar-) strings, Dylan was middle class, Jewish, the son of a shopkeeper from a remote Midwestern town. He wasn't even really called Bob Dylan. And far from losing touch with his parents, they were due in town a few days later to see their son perform at Carnegie Hall. One can only imagine what they thought of some of his wilder claims. We at least know how Dylan felt when he saw that issue of *Newsweek*: he is reported to have screamed.

11. Another Side

(1963-5)

DYLAN may well have screamed with frustration when he discovered *Newsweek* was publishing the true story of his roots, but if the revelation did any damage, it was minimal. Despite the folk scene's fierce insistence on authenticity, fans were still coming to his shows and buying his records. Dylan commented later, 'The press? I figured you lie to it.' Perhaps his fans felt the same. The time would come when Dylan and sections of his fan base parted company – but not on this point.

Newsweek's revelations were soon forgotten, overtaken by history. On November 22nd, President Kennedy was assassinated while visiting Dallas. The nation went into deep and prolonged mourning. In some ways the nation never recovered. The idealism the youthful figure of Kennedy embodied had received a terrible injury, and the country's mood would darken as the decade continued.

In January 1964, Dylan released his third album, *The Times They Are A-Changing*. It was more sombre than *Freewheelin'*, lacking the humour of its predecessors, a stark affair appropriate for a nation in

Another Side (1963-5)

mourning. For example, 'Ballad Of Hollis Brown' concerns a farmer so sunk in poverty and misery he shoots his family and himself to spare them worse.

In contrast, in February, Dylan and some friends took off to have some fun and to explore the country like Sal and Dean in Dylan's beloved novel *On The Road*. They set off on a three week cross-country road trip from New York to New Orleans in time for Mardi Gras, a wild carnival that celebrates the city's rich historical, ethnic and musical legacy.

One month after the release of *The Times They Are A-Changing*, Dylan was already hungry to pursue a new direction. He told his companions, 'Rimbaud's where it's at. That's the kind of writing I'm gonna do.'

On the trip, he worked on a new song, 'Mr Tambourine Man', which was quite unlike anything he had written before. It wasn't political, it wasn't comical, it wasn't a song of love lost or found. Dylan had already been hailed as a poet by his admirers but 'Mr Tambourine Man' signalled a new and experimental phase of lyricism. The song appears to describe a mysterious and spiritual experience. Little wonder many later attributed the song's inspiration to drug-taking, although it was finished before Dylan had his first experience of the hallucination-inducing drug LSD. If the Dylan singing the song is high on anything, it's most likely on being creative and the insights making music offers songwriters.

Bob Dylan

When Dylan began to play 'Mr Tambourine Man' in concert, it disturbed some of his more folkie fans. On first listening, the lyrics were almost abstract. The song so clearly lacked the concrete commitment to causes they prized. They were right to pick up on this. From here on out, Dylan was more and more uninterested in playing and writing protest songs.

A new song, 'My Back Pages', even explained the change in subject matter. Looking back on his short career only long enough to dismiss what he'd achieved so far, he sang that, although he was older, he felt more youthful. And it was true; his voice had dropped the sombre Okie inflections he absorbed from Woody Guthrie. There was a fresher quality to his singing voice and the material he was composing.

On the New Orleans road trip, Dylan heard two songs on the car radio that were to make an impact. First he tuned into The Animals' version of 'House Of The Rising Sun'. The Animals, an English electric group, had first heard the song covered by Dylan on his debut album. They worked up a full-band version that was a number one on both sides of the Atlantic and has been called the first folk-rock song. Folk-rock, which combined folk's style of lyrics with electric instrumentation, was popular over the next couple of years. Dylan was intrigued by the possibilities.

He felt the same widening of horizons when he heard his first Beatles song, 'I Want To Hold Your

Another Side (1963-5)

Hand'. He misheard the line, 'I can't hide, I can't hide, I can't hide' as 'I get high, I get high, I get high', and assumed – wrongly – that they too had been smoking the drug marijuana.

On June 9th, Dylan recorded his fourth album in one night. It was a complete contrast to his third. There were zany comedies like 'Motorpsycho Nitemare', where Dylan finds himself in an uncomfortable situation with a crazy farmer's daughter. In contrast, the love songs were sour and coloured by the end of his relationship with Suze. 'It Ain't Me, Babe' was a harder version of 'It's All Right, It Ain't Me Babe'. Recorded in one night, *Another Side Of Bob Dylan* is in retrospect a transitional album. The sound was still acoustic, but lyrically, Dylan was serving notice he was getting ready to move on.

The critical response was mixed. *Another Side Of Bob Dylan* won admirers but some of his oldest fans were unhappy about the lack of protest songs on the album. They dismissed it as indulgent.

Dylan began 1965 by returning to the recording studio to make his fifth album, *Bringing It All Back Home*. If there had been mutterings before, *Bringing It All Back Home* would cause more unhappiness amongst sections of Dylan's fans.

The lyrics were concentrating into ever greater streams of odd and arresting images. Some said Dylan's words were close to gibberish now. Certainly they weren't as straightforwardly understandable as

'Don't Think Twice, It's All Right' or 'Girl Of The North Country'. But you only have to listen to 'Blowin' In The Wind' or 'Hard Rain' to see right from the start Dylan had created mood by placing images next to each other; he was now taking this technique to a more daring place.

Dylan was determined to evade whatever expectations his fans and the media had of him and his music. To that end he readied himself to make the final break with his folkie audience. He was going to do the one thing he knew they could never forgive. He was going to go electric.

12. Going Electric

(1965)

FOR FOLKIES, electric music was loud and crass. By its very nature, it wasn't capable of poetry. It was commercial and so in folkies' opinion it could not say anything worth hearing, assuming you could hear lyrics over the racket the drums and guitars were creating. A rocker before he was a folkie, Dylan disagreed.

'Subterranean Homesick Blues' was the first fully electric song Dylan recorded. In the studio, Dylan and his musicians didn't rehearse before pushing the record button nor did they add extra musical parts once they'd run through the song. Dylan liked to fly by the seat of his pants. His musicians had to follow Dylan as best they could as he hit out, and they only had a few takes per song to nail it. Dylan was restless and throughout his career tended to drop songs if he couldn't get them to come out right in the recording studio fairly quickly. *Bringing It All Back Home* was recorded in three days.

As excited as Dylan was by his new electric sound, he hedged his bets by recording half the tracks on the album with an electric band and half acoustically accompanied by himself. The results exceeded expectation. In contradiction of the criticism soon to come his way, the *Bringing It All Back Home* songs proved a rock backing was no barrier to writing intelligent songs full of feeling.

In February 1965, Dylan began a co-headlining tour with Joan Baez. His relationship with her was cooling, and he had begun seeing other women, one of whom was Sara Lownds. Dylan would marry Lownds before the year ended. On April 26th, Dylan arrived in London to start a British tour accompanied by Baez.

He was filmed throughout the tour by young filmmaker D.A. Pennebaker. The result was the fly-on-the-wall rockumentary *Dont Look Back*. Pennebaker was to become famous as a documenter of rock stars and musical events. *Dont Look Back* is groundbreaking because rock stars have rarely allowed the level of access Pennebaker was granted. Dylan isn't always shown in a flattering light, which is refreshing to see today when rock stars routinely demand final approval of films about them. Sometimes the very biggest stars insist on the right to cut anything they don't like from interviews. Dylan has never been afraid of warts-and-all portraits, although he's grown more protective of his privacy over the years.

Baez was upset throughout the tour because Dylan wasn't returning a favour; having asked Dylan to guest during her shows, she expected he'd do the same for

Going Electric (1965)

her in the UK, where Dylan was the bigger draw. Dylan didn't want to become too associated with one person any more than he wanted to be known as a singer of just protest songs. He didn't invite her on stage and when she met him in the company of Sara Lownds, she knew the relationship was over.

While on this tour, Dylan and Pennebaker almost by accident invented the pop promotional video. The word iconic is overused in rock criticism but the sheer number of parodies and pastiches of Dylan's 'Subterranean Homesick Blues' video point to its importance. The video is simplicity itself. Dylan, filmed standing in an alley beside the Savoy Hotel where he was staying in London, holds and drops a sequence of placards upon which lyrics have been scrawled from the song, all in time to the music. Dylan's promo was a decade ahead of other acts and two decades before a channel that played only promos, MTV, went on air.

Although *Bringing It All Back Home* had been released in March, Dylan was still playing an all-acoustic set. For the time being, folkie fans could fool themselves the electric half of the record was a put-on, a joke, a passing phase. When Dylan flew home in June, he arrived to find the folk-rock band The Byrds at number one with a cover version of 'Mr Tambourine Man'. He took it as a further sign that his move into rock was the correct route to pursue.

He moved into the famous Chelsea Hotel in New

York, where Dylan Thomas, the poet he possibly took his stage name from, had spent the last days of his short life. He also continued his relationship with Sara Lownds. At the same time, Dylan came briefly into contact with the pop-artist Andy Warhol and Warhol's eccentric friends, performers, collaborators and hangers-on, known collectively as the Factory. Dylan, who was fascinated by freak shows and carnivals, hung around for a while.

Pop art was a movement in the visual arts that began in the United States in the 1950s. Pop artists were inspired by mass culture and advertising. Whereas art movements before pop art might stress their spiritual or intellectual qualities or the skill with which it was made, pop art celebrated its own supposed shallowness. In the process, it broadened the idea of what people considered art.

Warhol, who had worked in advertising, painted tins of Campbell's soup and made wooden sculptures of boxes of Brillo pads. It forced the art establishment to ask again just what art is. Warhol was deeply interested in popular music and soon would produce the first album by the experimental rock band the Velvet Underground. Dylan, who liked to paint, was at first attracted to Warhol's challenge to the art establishment and perhaps saw a connection with his own struggle with the folk scene. Dylan also was taking an underappreciated strand of popular culture – rock n' roll – and transforming it.

Going Electric (1965)

Dylan agreed to sit for one of Warhol's 'screen tests' – short films where the subject was invited to sit staring at the camera for minutes on end, nothing else. Despite what they had in common, Dylan wasn't entirely convinced by Warhol's art. Warhol gave him one of his Elvis Presley silk-screens. Unimpressed, Dylan swapped it with his manager for a sofa. In the 1980s, Grossman's wife sold the silkscreen for $720,000, much to the older, wiser Dylan's regret.

Dylan's acquaintance with Warhol is more significant for introducing him to Edie Sedgwick. Sedgwick was a New York socialite who appeared in a number of short, experimental films directed by Warhol. She was pretty and known for her unique sense of style, but she was fragile too, with growing drug problems. During 1965, Dylan had a brief affair with her. It has been said that she is 'Miss Lonely', the disgraced social climber Dylan addresses and dismisses so scathingly in 'Like A Rolling Stone'. Whether she is, Dylan isn't saying. What is certain is that with 'Like A Rolling Stone', Dylan would upset the conventions of rock music once more.

13. Goodbye to All That

(1965)

IN a body of work that enjoys numerous highlights, 'Like A Rolling Stone' stands tall as perhaps Dylan's definitive moment. He returned from his British tour feeling drained. He was even considering whether it wasn't time he quit music to do something else. He began to write something on his typewriter, he wasn't sure what at first, not lyrics, poetry perhaps, then as it grew and grew, a novel. When he looked over what he had written, 'this long piece of vomit, 20 pages long', as he called it, his mind began to work.

> 'Out of it I took 'Like a Rolling Stone' and made it as a single. And I'd never written anything like that before and it suddenly came to me that was what I should do. . . After writing that I wasn't interested in writing a novel, or a play. I just had too much, I want to write songs.'

On June 15th, Dylan went into Columbia's recording studios in New York. The first day failed to nail down a finished take; the next day, they got it. The song has a distinctive organ sound that was contributed by Al Kooper. Kooper bluffed his way into the studio as a 'stand-by' guitarist. The studio was full of guitarists, however. Instead, he somehow managed to get himself behind an organ where he bashed out the song's memorable swirling riff; Kooper described the sound as 'intuitive ineptitude'. Playing the track back, producer Tom Wilson wanted the organ track low in the mix; it was Dylan who insisted it have as prominent a position in the mix as it has. The organ sound on that record has been imitated many times.

At 5 minutes 59 seconds, 'Like A Rolling Stone' is twice as long as the then-average pop song. Dylan, who began by singing folk songs that had 15, 20 verses, wouldn't be contained. He took the risk radio wouldn't play the song. The single was released in July and, despite the record company's reservations, slowly climbed the charts until it reached number two, only kept off the top spot by the Beatles' 'Help'.

Days after the single was released Dylan travelled to the Newport Folk Festival. He planned on giving 'Like A Rolling Stone' its debut live performance at Newport. He must have realised how provocative this was. The folkies hated electric music and what it stood for in their mind. Did he really think he could win them over? Or did he want to provoke a definitive split with the people who had been his earliest supporters?

The day began with Pete Seeger playing a recording of a baby on stage, a peaceful note Dylan was itching to disturb. As Dylan took to the Newport stage flanked by his band, the event felt loaded with symbolism. One need only watch the Newport concert film *The Other Side Of The Mirror* to see how quickly Dylan had changed in the space of two years. At his first Newport appearance in 1963, Dylan had dressed scruffily in clothes not so different from his audience. He was skinny and hunched over his guitar and wore a nervous smile. Two years later, in his black leather jacket and tower of hair, Dylan looked every inch the rock star.

The band kicked into 'Maggie's Farm'. The meaning of the lyrics in this context – where Dylan refuses to work on the farm – don't need to be decoded: Dylan was serving notice he was quitting the folk scene to go his own way, do his own thing. Behind him, his guitarist played electrifying bluesy riffs. Seen today, it sounds scintillating, although the audience didn't have access to the remastered, cleaned-up sound DVD watchers can enjoy 40 years later.

Newport's sound system was primitive. It worked fine for folk artists but began to buzz and hiss as Dylan and his band overloaded it. Many in the audience could hear nothing but a racket. Once 'Maggie's Farm' finished, the booing began in earnest. Without pausing, Dylan rushed into 'Like A Rolling Stone' which the band struggled to hold together. Eventually, it petered out towards the close of the song. The band played one more song, 'It Takes A Lot To Laugh, It Takes A Train To Cry', and then left the stage to catcalls.

Goodbye to All That (1965)

There is a story, not true, but illustrative nonetheless, that Pete Seeger had threatened to sever with an axe the power line providing electricity to the instruments, so incensed was he said to be. For a long time, rock historians criticised the Newport audience for not being open to Dylan's thrilling vision of rock. Time has revealed this to be a somewhat simplistic explanation of the booing. Many, it appears, booed simply because the PA performed so badly. Seeger was furious not so much because the music angered him but because it sounded so awful. Others booed because the set was so short.

Indeed, if Dylan was so hated that night, watch the DVD performance and ask yourself – why is it when Peter Yarrow, the MC and one third of Peter, Paul and Mary, asks if the audience wants to see more of Dylan, he gets a big cheer?

It seems Yarrow, confronted by a sea of unhappy faces, decided on his own that Dylan should come back on stage and pacify them with a couple more numbers performed acoustically. This was galling to Dylan who was effectively forced back on stage after already having said everything he wanted to tell Newport. Borrowing an acoustic guitar, he ran back out, blinking. He'd be damned though if he did a protest song. He began with 'Mr Tambourine Man' and then concluded with another song whose message was clear: 'It's All Over Now, Baby Blue'. He left stage for a second time with cries of 'More' in his ears rather than booing.

Two years earlier at Newport he had been practically anointed leader of the scene during a group singalong of 'Blowin' In the Wind'; now he was being run out of town.

14. Crash

(1965-6)

THERE have been varied reports over the years about how Dylan felt about the booing at Newport, 1965. Some say he was indifferent, others that he was upset. Dylan has said little about it. His response at the time was to retreat behind his now-omnipresent shades and plan his next single, 'Positively 4th Street', a song that resembles 'Like A Rolling Stone' thematically and musically. The song is a bitter dismissal of former comrades.

Perhaps he was more stung than he let on.

Dylan was already recording what would be his second great album of 1965, *Highway 61 Revisited*. This collection of songs would be his first completely rock album.

'The folk music scene had been like a paradise that I had to leave, like Adam had to leave the garden.

It was just too perfect,' he wrote in his autobiography *Chronicles*.

His lyrics had moved further than ever from the protest songs that made him famous, although they honoured the folk tradition's love of a fantastical tale. The album ends with the 11-minute 'Desolation Row', a depiction of a semi-comic wasteland peopled by the likes of Cinderella and Anglo-American poet T.S. Eliot. It's a nightmarish world where everything is broken.

Dylan readied a band to tour. As a warm-up, he played Forest Hills Stadium, New York. The 15,000 seat arena was sold out. The format of the gig would remain unchanged for the following year. First, he played a 45-minute acoustic show. An interval followed, after which Dylan returned with his band to play a rock n' roll set. The reaction of the audience also, with exceptions, remained constant for the following year. They responded favourably enough to the acoustic set. But when the band came on, they booed. They slow handclapped and heckled. Many walked out.

After playing a couple of other large gigs, Dylan had to assemble a new band for the world tour he was planning. Some of the musicians playing with him, like Al Kooper, had been scared off by the booing; others had previous engagements to take care off. The new guys Dylan brought in to play with him came as a unit. The Hawks were a real rock n' roll band that had played every dive and two-bit saloon on the road during a long apprenticeship. They were masters of raucous, wall-trembling noise. As confirmed rockers they knew little about folk and not much more about Dylan himself – which suited Dylan just fine.

Dylan married Sara Lownds on November 22nd at a quiet service. Sara was pregnant when she married. Dylan kept news of his impending fatherhood and the marriage itself secret for several months following the ceremony. The news came as an unwelcome surprise to some girlfriends. Edie Sedgwick for example was under the impression not only that she and Dylan were an item but that they would be making a film together.

Dylan travelled to Nashville to record his next album, *Blonde On Blonde*, arriving at the studio on Valentine's Day, 1966. Nashville was an interesting choice, given its association then as now with country music. Country music in the 1960s was seen by the sort of hipsters who liked Dylan as music for rednecks and cavemen.

The crew of seasoned session musicians assembled to capture Dylan's shimmering take on blues-rock were puzzled by the singer-songwriter. He hired them to sit idle in the studio for hours, sometimes well into the night, while he wrote songs on his typewriter in another room. When he felt ready, he came into the studio, gave the musicians their instructions and set off. Songs were recorded in one or two takes, with musicians having no idea how long the track was meant to go on for. On one song, the epic 'Sad Eyed Lady Of The Lowlands', the musicians found themselves playing for over 11 minutes wondering when Dylan was going to give them the signal to wind down the music.

For album opener, 'Rainy Day Woman #12 & 35', Dylan wanted the sound of a ragged marching band. To that end, he got half the band drunk, and then he made them swap instruments. After detailing in the verses the many crimes a person could be stoned for, Dylan declares, 'Everybody must get stoned', an unsubtle drug reference that was no barrier to the song climbing to number two in the US charts, his bestselling single.

In 1969, Dylan was asked how important drug taking was to the making of *Blonde On Blonde*. He told his interviewer: 'No, not the writing of them, but it did keep me up there to pump 'em out.' In this period, his banned substance of choice was amphetamines, which gave him the energy to write and record for days with little rest. In part it contributes to the sound of the album, what Dylan described as 'that thin mercury sound'. A double LP, *Blonde On Blonde* is the perfect summation of the second phase of Dylan's career.

The new album wouldn't be released until May. Before then, Dylan was contracted to play a world

Crash (1965-6)

tour and so he and the Hawks set off. They stopped off in Australia on their way to Europe. The concerts in Britain were to prove the most contentious of the tour outside America.

British audiences were divided as to the merits of Dylan's new direction. Largely, they enjoyed the acoustic section, only for all hell to break loose when Dylan returned to the stage with the Hawks. Violent emotions were roused. The infamous 'Judas!' incident at Manchester Free Trade Hall goaded Dylan into replying in the best way he knew how, a howling version of 'Like A Rolling Stone'. Afterwards, Dylan's documentary crew interviewed concertgoers. One young man, face red with anger, looks directly at the camera. 'He wants shooting,' he says with conviction.

Dylan was drinking, smoking, and taking drugs more than ever. By the time he returned to America, he was thin, wasted-looking, unwell. He needed time to recover. Yet he had more dates lined up for later in the year. In addition, he had signed a book contract to write a volume which had only been completed as far as its title, *Tarantula*. He had agreed to edit a new tour movie. And there were plans to go back into the studio and record another album. Dylan, however, didn't look physically capable.

By July, Dylan, his wife and new son had left New York to go upstate, to Woodstock, an artist's colony founded in the nineteenth century, where his manager Albert Grossman also lived. The idea was to get some rest. On Friday July 29th, something happened, something that has never entirely been cleared up. While riding a motorbike, Dylan fell and had some sort of accident that required medical attention. How serious was it? By the time the news got out, the accident was reported to be very serious. Some said he couldn't walk anymore. Some said he was dead.

15. Down in the Basement

(1966-8)

DYLAN'S motorcycle accident not only marks a natural concluding point to another phase in his career, but so shrouded are the actual circumstances it has acquired a mythic quality. It's almost a pity then to report the accident wasn't nearly as serious as speculation at the time would have it.

While we're still uncertain even where exactly the accident took place, the best guess is it happened while Dylan was driving his motorbike round Albert Grossman's estate in Woodstock. At the hospital, he was found to have cracked vertebrae, which is painful but not life-threatening, although the diagnosis was possibly complicated by the poor physical condition Dylan was in at the time of the accident. It did at least free Dylan of his immediate obligations. Possibly he was happy to let rumours about his health fly out of control; the worse the state he was said to be in, the longer the break he could take.

After a hectic four years during which Dylan had resorted to drugs and alcohol to keep himself upright, he was glad to take an extended holiday. But no one, perhaps not even Dylan himself, could have anticipated how long he would retreat from the public eye. Today we're used to rock musicians taking off several years between albums. In the latter half of the sixties, it was simply unheard of for a star to disappear for 18 months. It only excited the rumour mill more. What was Dylan doing in Woodstock?

His fans might well have been disappointed to learn Dylan was enjoying being a family man. In 1986 Dylan told the playwright, collaborator and in this instance his interviewer Sam Shepard that after the motorcycle accident, 'I started thinkin' about how short life is. I'd just lay there listenin' to birds chirping. Kids playing in the neighbour's yard or rain falling by the window. I realised how much I'd missed.'

Dylan hadn't stopped songwriting, just recording and touring. He invited the Hawks to Woodstock. They hired a house in nearby West Saugerties which they called Big Pink because of the colour of its facade. Dylan and the Hawks soon worked out a routine. Every day Dylan would drive over to Big Pink, arriving at noon, when he would spend some time writing lyrics on his typewriter. Afternoons were spent jamming out new songs or covering Dylan favourites. A reel-to-reel tape recorder captured the sessions.

The harvest of music that followed, dubbed *The Basement Tapes*, was a fantastic collection of songs. Even more incredibly, despite their quality, most of the songs even to this day have never been officially released.

Down in the Basement (1966-8)

What do *The Basement Tapes* sound like? The first thing to bear in mind is that the tapes were never meant to be heard by the public. They were recorded strictly for Dylan and the Hawks' amusement. You hear the sound of a band relaxing after a year of touring and recording. Many of the songs have humorous lyrics, others are more cryptic, sometimes both.

Dylan had been reading the Bible, with the consequence some of the songs have a parable-like quality. Others are earthier. As Greil Marcus put in it in *Invisible Republic*, his book on *The Basement Tapes*, the songs are 'pitched somewhere between the confessional and the bawdy house'.

During Dylan's time out, the world continued to spin. In April Israel fought and won against its Middle Eastern neighbours in the Six Day War. Greece was taken over by a military dictatorship. Boxer Muhammad Ali refused the draft and was stripped of his world heavyweight championship title as punishment. The United States Supreme Court declared state laws banning inter-racial marriage unconstitutional. Homosexuality was decriminalised and abortion legalised in Britain. Nigeria invaded its rebel province of Biafra; many people died in the conflict. A series of race riots spread across America. In September, Radio One was launched in the UK. The following month hero of the Cuban revolution, Che Guevara, was captured in Bolivia organising another revolution; soon after, he was executed.

The Beatles released *Sgt Pepper's Lonely Hearts Club Band* in June, 1967. With this album, the Beatles perfected the art of using the studio itself as an instrument. The tracks were ornate, deeply conceived and executed, often at some cost financially. In the wake of its release, *Pepper* was widely imitated.

Dylan appeared, perhaps consciously, to go in the opposite direction, to make his music simpler, barer. There is a ghostly, half-finished, outside-of-time sound to *The Basement Tapes*. Some of its numbers feel as if they could have been recorded anytime in the past century.

Dylan initially had no greater ambition for *The Basement Tapes* than to have fun. Eventually, once he realised the quality of new originals like 'Quinn The Eskimo (The Mighty Quinn)', 'I Shall Be Released', 'Tears Of Rage', and 'This Wheel's On Fire', he decided to have a selection of the taped songs pressed onto record and shopped around musicians and managers to see if they cared to cover the unreleased material. Many did, and many – like Manfred Mann who recorded 'Quinn The Eskimo' – had huge hits with the tracks. 'I Shall Be Released', a song about a prisoner looking forward to leaving his cell for good, would eventually become Dylan's third most covered song.

Not everyone liked what they heard coming from Big Pink. A future critic described *The Basement Tapes* as 'deserters' songs' because of their lack of commitment to chronicling a troubled age. Many if not most serious musicians felt obliged to talk about their times. And here was the man who started it all turning his face away just when he was needed the most.

When Dylan returned to a recording studio proper in 1968, the album he produced couldn't have been more different to *Blonde On Blonde*. *John Wesley Harding* was recorded in six weeks and has a notably more sober sound. The surprising images and the withering sarcasm were gone and replaced by something, on the surface at least, simpler.

The distance between Dylan and his musical peers was further than it ever had been. And about to get further.

16. Losing It

(1968-74)

DYLAN'S next move convinced many of his fans that he had gone mad in Woodstock. He decamped to Nashville, not to record a sequel to *Blonde On Blonde*, but to record an album of country songs. Fans were shocked. They thought of country as the music of the sort of right-wing hick who supports the Vietnam War.

Dylan was once again ahead of the curve. Within a few years, the biggest, most lucrative musical trend in America would be country rock. The band The Eagles would sell out arena after arena playing radio-friendly takes on country. At the time Dylan's *Nashville Skyline* appeared in 1969, the only others doing something similar were his old camp followers The Byrds.

Dylan further unnerved fans by singing the entire album in a mildly strangulated voice reminiscent of his early influence, American country star Hank Williams. Amongst Dylanologists, *Nashville Skyline* does not enjoy a good critical reputation. It's invariably snubbed as a minor work. Yet while Dylan's hardcore fans might never have embraced the album, the public did. Until the release of his *Greatest Hits Vol. II* in 1971, *Nashville Skyline* was Dylan's best-selling album. It sold more than *Highway 61 Revisited* and *Blonde On Blonde*.

After returning to public life, Dylan's Woodstock home was invaded by fans and weirdos, pilgrims and nomads. His address had been reported in the press and now the crazies were knocking on his door. One time he returned home to find a pair of fans in his bed. The pressure on him had not relaxed despite his year off and country music detour.

Though he was not quite 30 yet, Dylan was by now father to five children, four his own and one step-daughter. He and his family moved back to New York, to a townhouse on McDougall Street in Greenwich Village. His choice was prompted by nostalgia for the early days of his career. It was a mistake. Crowds of hippies, radicals and malcontents would mill about on the street outside making normal life difficult.

The worst offender was a 25-year-old college drop-out called A.J. Weberman, the self-appointed leader of the Dylan Liberation Front. He stood outside Dylan's home with a sign reading 'Free Bob Dylan From Himself'. He objected to what he saw as Dylan's rejection of his early radicalism. By 1971, Weberman had graduated to stealing Dylan's trash in order to prove his theory that Dylan was a heroin addict (Weberman gave this 'technique' the name 'garbology'). He was convinced Dylan had already admitted his addiction in code in his recent lyrics. For Dylan's 30th birthday, he sent him a cake with candles in the shape of hypodermic syringes. Dylan for his part stuffed his bin bags with soiled nappies.

What mattered most to Dylan now was not changing 'the whole music scene' (he'd already done that at least twice). What mattered most was getting the world off his and his family's back.

Nashville Skyline completed one rethink of his image. Dylan wanted to push it further. His next album, *Self Portrait*, was initially conceived of as an album of cover versions. He was in dispute with Albert Grossman over royalties arising from songs he wrote himself. An album of cover versions would deprive Grossman of more money (Dylan soon sacked Grossman). As a covers album, *Self Portrait* is a forerunner to his nineties covers collections *Good As I Been To You* and *World Gone Wrong*, though where those albums have a stark authenticity, *Self Portrait* is composed of syrupy country renderings.

It had come to Dylan's attention around this time that his *Basement Tapes* had been bootlegged and was being sold by enterprising fans. Today, thanks to the internet and file-sharing, we're used to the notion of getting our hands on unreleased songs, alternative versions, and live covers by our favourite bands. By the sixties, jazz and opera fans had traded bootlegs for some time, but Dylan was the first rock star to be bootlegged.

Losing It (1968-74)

The key Dylan bootleg in the late 1960s was *Great White Wonder*, a collection of early acoustic material and *Basement Tapes* songs; it was even eventually reviewed by *Rolling Stone* magazine. Intrigued, Dylan toyed with the idea of releasing his own 'bootleg'. With that in mind, he included amongst the covers on *Self Portrait* some original material and live tracks recorded with the Hawks (who were now recording their own albums under the name of The Band; their first Dylan-influenced album, *Music From Big Pink*, was released in 1968 to acclaim).

Released in 1970, *Self Portrait* has been called 'one of the most despised and ridiculed records of the past 30 years'. Dylan's fans were left scratching their heads. To them it didn't seem so much a change of direction as a dereliction of duty. *Doesn't he want to lead us anymore?* they asked. Evidently not.

Self Portrait certainly gathered the harshest reviews of his career. During his 'going electric' phase he had encountered fierce resistance from audiences but hip critics had seen what he was doing. Now even they turned against him. But if he was trying to get rid of fans, he didn't do a great job. *Self Portrait* went gold in America and was even a number one album in the UK.

In this period, Dylan was content. One only need listen to the music to hear he had taken his foot off the accelerator creatively. Happiness writes white, they say. It's a cliché, but does at least identify why his material at the start of the 1970s wasn't as compelling as his earlier work.

As the seventies progressed Dylan himself appeared for the first time in a while to be troubled by his lack of creativity. In 1974, he embarked upon a major tour for the first time since 1966 backed by the Band, now successful in their own right, to promote the album they made together, *Planet Waves*. With pricey tickets, the shows were a money-spinner. The booing of 1966 was but a memory now. Yet Dylan later said he hated 'every minute' of this tour. He was tempted by old bad habits. He was drinking a lot and, it was rumoured, seeing other women on the road.

His marriage was in trouble, not that one would have guessed from his lyrics on *Planet Waves*. Lyrical clues as to what was taking place in his private life would have to wait until 1975 when he would release an album that, while giving voice to doubts about his relationship with Sara, silenced the doubts about what had happened to his singular talent.

17. Rolling Thunder

(1974-5)

WITH 1975's *Blood On The Tracks*, Dylan not only reclaimed his gift for lyric-writing; he might even have recorded his greatest album. His achievement is all the greater once you realise the subject that dominates the album – the disintegration of his marriage. It's one thing to write about civil rights or to mock your critics; writing about the mother of your children is quite another matter.

It would be an overstatement to say *Blood On The Tracks* is entirely 'about' Dylan and Sara's misfortunes. Dylan wasn't given to penning true confessions. Since his early days, his best lyrics had balanced emotion against a strong literary conceit. While many of the tracks deal with the fall-out of failing relationships, Dylan rarely indulges in straight exercises in autobiography. For example, 'Lily, Rosemary, And The Jack Of Hearts' from *Blood On The Tracks* is one of Dylan's tall tales set in a frontier town, which equates romantic folly with criminal activity.

How did *Blood On The Tracks* come to be recorded? It begins with Dylan's growing estrangement from Sara. Looking for something to absorb his energies, Dylan returned to his passion for painting and drawing. In the Spring of 1974, he enrolled as a pupil in art teacher Norman Raeben's classes in New York. Raeben's lessons seemed to light a fire in Dylan's imagination. It can be heard on *Blood On The Tracks* on its first track, 'Tangled Up In Blue', where Dylan takes an almost Cubist approach to his subject by distorting the timeline of the story the song tells. Here, past and present sit next to each other in the same way Cubist paintings break up objects and reassemble them.

Raeben's ideas about perception and reality didn't just have an effect on Dylan's drawn and sung art. He unwittingly unmoored the Dylans' marriage. As Dylan later said, 'It changed me. I went home after that first day and my wife never did understand me ever since that day. That's when our marriage started breaking up. She never knew what I was talking about, what I was thinking about, and I couldn't possibly explain it.'

In July 1974, stories began to appear in the press reporting the Dylans' marriage was in trouble. The same stories linked him to a number of other women. By September, Dylan began work in New York on what would become *Blood On The Tracks*. The songs were subdued, sometimes little more than Dylan accompanying himself on his guitar, the lyrics amongst the best he had ever set down.

When the album was released in January, 1975,

fans and critics were united in hailing *Blood On The Tracks* as one of his best. It reached number one on the American Billboard album charts, number four in the UK.

Dylan evidently found the praise *Blood On The Tracks* earned troubling. 'A lot of people tell me they enjoy that album. It's hard for me to relate to that. I mean, you know, people enjoying that type of pain?'

In June, Dylan read *The Sixteenth Round* by Rubin Carter. Once a contender for middleweight champion of the world, Carter was by 1975 incarcerated, sentenced to four consecutive life sentences for the murder of three people shot during a bar robbery in New Jersey. Carter denied responsibility. The evidence against him collected by the police was circumstantial or unreliable. After the guilty verdict was pronounced, the judge decided not to impose the death sentence, a sign, perhaps, that he had some doubts of his own whether Carter was the killer. A campaign to get Carter's sentence overturned was launched which attracted, amongst other celebrities, Muhammad Ali. Carter sent a copy of his autobiography to Dylan because of his early involvement with the civil rights movement. After reading it, Dylan visited him in Rahway State Prison, New Jersey. He said afterwards, 'This man's philosophy and my philosophy were running on the same road.'

Still, he wasn't sure what to do. Write a song? Theatre director and lyricist Jacques Levy, with whom he was collaborating, encouraged him to pen the song. Dylan had begun his writing career seriously with 'The Ballad Of Emmett Till', the story of an African American who suffered rough justice. For the first time in nearly a decade, Dylan found himself composing a protest song, 'Hurricane'. He had some doubts.

'He was just filled with all these feelings about Hurricane,' Levy said. 'He couldn't make the first step. I think the first step was putting the song in a total storytelling mode. I don't remember whose idea it was to do that. But really, the beginning of the song is like stage directions, like what you would read in a script: "Pistol shots ring out in a barroom night. . . Here comes the story of the Hurricane". Boom! Titles. You know, Bob loves movies, and he can write these movies that take place in eight to ten minutes, yet seem as full or fuller than regular movies.' (Rubin Carter was released, charges dropped, in 1988.)

Rather than rest on his laurels, Dylan returned to Columbia's New York studios in July 1975 with a strong batch of new songs. *Desire* is marked by more career-best material. Any doubt that *Blood On The Tracks* was some sort of fluke, a one-off inspired by personal woes, was dispelled.

On July 31st, Sara Dylan arrived unannounced at *Desire's* second session. As it happened Dylan was about to record a song called 'Sara', a heartfelt plea for his wife to forgive him and to take him back. For

Rolling Thunder (1974-5)

a lyricist who had always preferred to channel events in his personal life into allegories, 'Sara' was extraordinarily naked, and all the more powerful for it. Here, Dylan asks his wife to remember their children, the holidays they took together, even how he wrote 'Sad Eyed Lady Of The Lowlands' for her in the Chelsea Hotel (bit of a fib; he wrote it in Nashville at the studio). The song ends with Dylan imploring his wife not to end the marriage.

Sara, who was in the studio watching her husband perform, was stunned and touched by the song, which did indeed affect a reconciliation between the pair. The song was completed in one take and it is that version that rounds off *Desire*.

With the album finished and not slated to appear before January 1976, Dylan began to recruit musicians for the greatest tour of his life. Dylan invited many old friends to go back on the road with him. He asked Ramblin' Jack Elliott, the Byrds' Roger McGuinn, Allen Ginsberg – and Joan Baez.

Although Baez and Dylan's relationship in the sixties had not ended happily, she accepted his invitation. Each night on the tour they sang several songs together and it was clear there was still a spark of sexual chemistry between them.

The Rolling Thunder Revue began on October 30th, 1975. The concept for the show was one Dylan had had for some time. He wanted 'an old-timey medicine show'. In the collaborative spirit that produced *Desire*, Dylan didn't want to be the centre of the show, not all the time. The idea was that the band would be onstage the entire night with the main acts sliding on and off stage unannounced as the evening progressed. Ramblin' Jack might start the night off with Baez or McGuinn joining later. Dylan would come onstage and play guitar on his friends' sets without signalling his presence. Often it took the audience a little while to realise the headliner was present. Dylan would play his set, leave and return before leading the entire cast through a final song.

When the show reached Lowell, Massachusetts, a few days later, Dylan began to come on stage with his face covered in white make up. Theories abounded, as they do whenever Dylan does almost anything. Some thought it was a reference to the minstrel tradition. Others thought that with his face painted a ghastly pale, he was playing a sort of skull-faced Death who presides over the carnivalesque show as he presides over life. Dylan himself explained that with so many people on stage, he needed something to stand out. He also told the young Bruce Springsteen backstage in New Haven, 'I saw it in a movie once.'

18. Falling From Grace

(1976-87)

WHEN *Desire* appeared at the start of 1976, it went to number one on the Billboard album charts, number three in the UK. The second leg of the Rolling Thunder Revue began in April, 1976. Curiously, this second leg was underappreciated by audiences who could barely rouse themselves. Some of the energy and buzz about the show leaked away.

Dylan himself was in trouble. After his reconciliation with Sara, their marriage had run into trouble once more. He was drinking, seeing other women, and unhappy.

The marriage was finished. Divorce proceedings began and were finalised in June 1977. It got bitter. He was separated from his family. His new material was uninspired.

On November 17th, 1978, while on stage in San Diego, Dylan picked up a small silver cross. By the time the show reached Tuscon, Dylan sat alone in his hotel room, his spirits low, staring at the cross. By his own account, he had a vision. 'I had a born-again experience,' he told *The LA Times*. 'Jesus put his hand on me. It was a physical thing. I felt it all over me. I felt my body tremble. The glory of the Lord knocked me down and picked me up.'

In the late 1970s, there was something of a vogue for Christianity in rock, perhaps as a reaction to the excesses of the sixties and seventies. After his vision, Dylan converted to Christianity. His family, who were raised Jewish, were understandably mystified.

Dylan being Dylan, he couldn't merely convert and sit on it. Swiftly he wrote a whole new batch of Christian rock songs. He travelled to the legendary Muscle Shoals Sound Studio in Alabama to record the album, and recruited Jerry Wexler, producer of soul legends Ray Charles, Aretha Franklin, and Wilson Pickett. Wexler hadn't realised Dylan wanted to make a 'born-again' album when he signed on. When Dylan tried to convert him, Wexler politely told him, 'Bob, you're dealing with a sixty-two-year-old confirmed Jewish atheist. Let's make an album.'

The resulting album, *Slow Train Coming*, was great. Dylan's music had rarely sounded so good, thanks to the crack musicians Wexler recruited. Wexler called it 'immaculate funk'. Nevertheless, the album received some of the most dismissive reviews of Dylan's career.

Dylan continued to record Christian rock songs, not nearly as good as *Slow Train Coming's* efforts, and in the process lost a sizeable portion of his core

Falling From Grace (1976-87)

audience. In concert, he stopped playing his old songs; he was only interested in playing his born-again compositions. Arenas were half-empty or worse. He began sermonising on stage as if he was a gospel minister. He was booed for the first time since going electric.

By 1981, Dylan was starting to come out of his Christian period. He began to open his live set to older songs again. He also began to write songs with non-religious subjects. But it would take almost ten years for Dylan to recapture his former glory. For good reason, the eighties were called Dylan's 'lost decade'.

For much of the 1980s, Dylan could barely put a foot right. He didn't even appear capable of judging 'how good' his own songs were. It became almost standard practice for him to consign to the vaults the best songs recorded during sessions, weakening albums that needed all the help they could get. Album sales got progressively worse.

Although Dylan himself had a bad decade, in some ways the eighties were to prove the culmination of what he and his peers had begun in the sixties. By the eighties, pop stars were expected to speak out and take stands on the big issues of the day. Even a bubblegum pop act like George Michael's Wham! played a miners' benefit concert.

After a period when hostilities had eased during the seventies, the Cold War was as icy as ever, prompting many musicians and young people to join groups like the Campaign for Nuclear Disarmament (CND). The biggest event of the decade where pop stars showed what they could do when they organised themselves was Live Aid, a massive trans-Atlantic concert featuring the biggest names of the day playing to raise money for the starving in Ethiopia.

Dylan, as the one-time 'voice of a generation', was invited to headline the Philadelphia leg of Live Aid. It was a disaster. Dylan, who spent the day drinking instead of rehearsing, was shambolic. Before a global TV audience of millions he looked sweaty and nervous. The final nail in the coffin came when Dylan said, 'I'd just like to say I hope that some of the money that's raised for the people in Africa, maybe they could just take a little bit of – maybe one or two million maybe – and use it, say, to pay the. . . er. . . pay the mortgages on some of the farms. . . what the farmers owe to the banks.'

As bad as the economic situation might have been for some farmers in America at the time, they weren't starving like the people of Ethiopia. It was a poorly judged remark.

Dylan began to dress differently around this period: leather trousers, big hair, dangly earrings. Some attribute this flashy new look to his backing singer Carolyn Dennis. On June 4th, 1986, Dylan married her in secret. So successful was he in keeping the secret, and getting friends and family to

Falling From Grace (1976-87)

stay quiet too, the public didn't learn he had married again until the publication in 2001 of Howard Sounes' biography of Dylan, *Down The Highway*. Dylan also managed to keep out of the press the birth of a daughter.

Musically, he appeared to give up in the latter part of the 1980s. He admitted as much. 'If the records I'm making only sell a certain amount anyway, then why should I take so long putting them together?' The albums released during this phase of his career are unexceptional, occasionally embarrassing. 'Sometimes I think I've done this too long,' Dylan confided to an interviewer. 'I can understand why Rimbaud quit writing poetry when he was 19.'

He reached something of a crisis point on October 5th, 1987, when he found he couldn't sing moments before going on stage in Locarno, Switzerland. He was disconnected from the songs that made him famous. He felt lost. But he heard himself inside his head saying, 'I'm determined to stand, whether God will deliver me or not.' He was able finally to go on stage but he realised something would have to change.

19. World Gone Right

(1987-2010)

AFTER injuring his hand, Dylan found himself stuck at home at the end of 1987. To his surprise, after a long layoff he felt moved to write songs again, starting in December of that year. Early in 1988, U2 singer Bono visited Dylan at his home, where his host showed him the lyrics he'd been working on. Bono urged him to record them, but Dylan was unsure, having lost the pleasure he took in the recording process. Bono hooked Dylan up with his producer, Daniel Lanois, they met, and plans were made to record an album in 1989.

Determined to reconnect with his own musical legacy, Dylan dispensed with the large touring band he'd been playing with to concentrate on guitar, bass, and drums, the essentials. He debuted his new live sound on June 7th, 1988, at California's Concord Pavilion.

This was the beginning of what has become known as the Never Ending Tour. Since it began Dylan has toured the world with a frequency that would exhaust many a younger man. It's become a hallmark of these tours that old songs are often arranged to an almost unrecognisable degree; this is no golden-oldies nostalgia trip.

Dylan and Lanois began recording together in March, 1989. Lanois' production is known for being atmospheric, an effect he liked to foster by recording in unusual locations. Lanois installed a portable studio in a Victorian mansion in New Orleans. Lanois filled the house with moss and alligator heads.

By Dylan's own account, the sessions were sometimes ill-tempered. Dylan had become lazy in the studio over the years, picked up bad habits, and Lanois wouldn't stand for it. Like Jerry Wexler, he was a producer unafraid of telling Dylan what to do and where he was going wrong. By the time they reached the end of the sessions, it was clear Dylan had recorded a very fine album, *Oh Mercy*, his best since *Desire* in 1976.

In the twenty years since Dylan recorded *Oh Mercy*, he has struggled to maintain quality control. *Oh Mercy* pointed the way for him to go next, but it would take another half-wasted decade before he listened to himself. *Oh Mercy's* follow-up *Under A Blood Sky* was an underwhelming, guest-star heavy album which almost completely ignores the lessons he had relearned during *Oh Mercy*. It was as if he couldn't be bothered. With his second wife divorcing him, perhaps he wasn't.

Inspiration dried up. Writer's block descended once more. Instead of recording new material, he covered a selection of traditional songs, 'the music that is true for me', in his home studio accompanying himself on acoustic guitar and harmonica. The material ranged from the sixteenth century to the thirties. The resulting album, *Good As I Been To You,* was released the week Bill Clinton was elected President. Good critical notices encouraged Dylan to record another album of covers, *World Gone Wrong,* the following year. Of these songs he wrote:

> These old songs are my lexicon and my prayer book. You can find all my philosophy in these old songs. Hank Williams singing 'I Saw The Light'. . . That would be pretty close to my religion. The rabbis, priests, and ministers all do very well. But my belief system is more rugged and comes more from out of the old spiritual songs than from any of the established religious attempts at overcoming the devil.

World Gone Wrong reached number 70 in the Billboard charts, his worst ever album position. Influential DJ John Peel played Dylan on his show for the first time since the 1960s, but, generally, the opinion was these two covers albums, released at the height of grunge, confirmed Dylan was now a relic, an irrelevance, at best a heritage act.

This was unfair. With hindsight, we can see that

World Gone Right (1987-2010)

Dylan – by reconnecting with the source of his inspiration – was preparing for his next artistic revival. The signs were promising. He cut down on his drinking in the mid-1990s. He hooked up with Daniel Lanois again and the rumours were his new songs were good. The comeback was gearing up – then Dylan almost died.

In May 1997, Dylan was admitted to hospital suffering chest pains. He had *pericarditis*, an inflammation of the sac around the heart caused by a fungal infection. It is painful and if untreated, fatal. The fungus is found in soil enriched with bird droppings. It is suspected Dylan picked up the infection while motorbiking through the south after a storm blew traces of the fungus into the air (when is Dylan going to learn he and motorcycles do not have a good history together?). Dylan said, 'I really thought I'd be seeing Elvis soon.'

Dylan had only just completed recording sessions for his album, *Time Out Of Mind*, when he fell ill, and it's fascinating to consider what the reaction to it would have been if he had died. For the album is itself preoccupied with mortality and doubt about the choices one makes in life. Dylan's voice by now was a ruined croon – thanks to overwork, cigarettes, booze and age – and perfect for this album.

Time Out Of Mind sold over two million copies and won an Album of the Year Grammy. It began a resurgence in Dylan's critical fortunes and with it, a renewed interest in him and his life story. These past ten years have been Dylan's most consistently successful period commercially and creatively since the mid-seventies.

Like those great final albums by his friend, the late Johnny Cash, the music Dylan has released since *Time Out Of Mind* – *Love And Theft* (2001), *Modern Times* (2005), *Together Through Life* (2009) – betray a keen awareness of a mind travelling through the last quarter of his life. While the mood can get dark at times, Dylan also approaches his subject with humour, fatalism, and a romantic sense of what is still possible in the time left.

You have to applaud Dylan's gutsiness, for sticking it out during many prolonged periods when he had all but lost faith in his talent. In the sixties, he faced down his critics. Since then he has had to face down a tougher foe, himself. He should be an inspiration to anyone who has doubted they can keep going in a field of work they once loved but which has lost its shine for them.

EPILOGUE
Things Have Changed

FOR DYLAN FANS, the past decade has felt like a celebration the likes of which you would have never thought possible at points during the nineties. He released four albums, two of which reached number one on the US Billboard album chart; he published a memoir, *Chronicles: Volume One*; hosted the acclaimed radio show *Theme Time Radio Hour*; contributed to an epic documentary about his early career, *No Direction Home*, which was directed by arguably America's greatest living film director, Martin Scorsese; had a biopic made inspired by his 'lives', *I'm Not There* (2007); and toured constantly, playing over a thousand shows. He even won an Oscar for Best Original Song with 'Things Have Changed' in 2000.

His passion remains first and last music. You need only listen to his acclaimed *Theme Time Radio Show* to hear he still gets a kick out of sharing his enthusiasm for music, old and new. His commitment to the Never Ending Tour proves he still has a thirst for taking his music to the people.

Dylan's behaviour is as pleasingly puzzling as

always. While in town to play Liverpool's Echo Arena on May 1st 2009, he took a tourist bus trip out to the house in Woolton where John Lennon grew up. In July, while on tour in New Jersey, he decided to visit Bruce Springsteen's old home, again by himself. He was picked up by police in Long Beach in the pouring rain after they received calls about 'an old scruffy man acting suspiciously'. The 20-year-old rookie cop who stopped him had no idea who he was. 'I wasn't sure if he came from one of our hospitals or something. He was acting very suspiciously.' When Dylan couldn't produce ID, she put him in the back of her police car and took him back to his hotel to check his story.

* * *

Washington DC on the night of February 10th, 2010, was far snowier than the bitter weather that greeted the 19-year-old Bob Dylan when he arrived in New York in 1961. Hundreds of flights were cancelled. Millions of Americans on the east coast were effectively housebound until the cold spell passed. Still, Dylan made it into town somehow. He was a boy from the north country. Snow didn't scare him. Wasn't his producer's pseudonym Jack Frost?

I've sometimes wondered about that. Was 'Jack Frost' chosen randomly? Or did it connect with some memory of the weather he grew up with in Hibbing? Some familial memory perhaps of the elements that froze the Russian countryside his grandparents fled a century earlier. Or was it a nod to that night he first arrived in New York seeking. . . what? Fame? Fortune? Dylan always gave the impression such things didn't interest him. Did he want to change the world like all ambitious young men are supposed to want to? Again, he denies it now. Maybe it really was about the music all along. As always Dylan generates questions like Catherine Wheels spin out sparks.

No man can deny his past, not even Dylan. He learned that to his cost in 1963 when *Newsweek* chased down his Hibbing childhood. And the night of February 10th, 2010 was in part about acknowledging an aspect of his past that he's often affected to deny, to claim it was a passing phase, a career move, even some sort of joke.

Dylan was in Washington to play a celebration of civil rights music at the White House at the invitation of President Barack Obama. He wasn't the first President Dylan had played for. But this time it was different, for Obama, the United States' first black President, owes much to the civil rights movement of the fifties and the sixties. And the civil rights movement owes much to the music that sustained it during some dark and long years.

In *Chronicles*, Dylan says he's not a political person, and suggests he doesn't even vote. I wonder if that held true in 2008. Dylan has a mixed race daughter of his own. I'd bet all my bootlegs he was listening that November night Obama made his acceptance speech and remembered another speech he heard in Washington 45 years earlier when he was Martin Luther King's warm-up act. The dream had come true.

So they were all there, friends, comrades, and lovers. Joan Baez, grey-haired, still beautiful, ran through 'We Shall Overcome' one more time, still fighting, now for gay rights, the environment, Iraq. Motown legend Smokey Robinson spoke to the 100 black teenagers drawn from all over the country about what segregation was like. Robinson is the man Dylan once called 'America's greatest living poet', which was a gracious thing for the true champ to say. Not on the guest list but there nonetheless, there were the ghosts of others who had fallen on the long path to freedom: Medgar Evers, Emmett Till, Martin Luther King Jnr.

Finally, it was Dylan's turn to sing. There were many songs he might have chosen. In the end, he began plucking the chords to 'The Times They Are A-Changing', a subdued but persuasive arrangement. Dylan, Live Aid notwithstanding, isn't without a sense of occasion.

The lyrics demand that politicians do not get in the way of change. Originally the song referred to civil rights. A new interpretation was there to be made, that those opposing Obama's modest health-care reforms should re-examine their position.

The important thing is the song had found its

mark, as much as it had in a different context almost half a century earlier. If the decades have proved anything it is that Dylan's back pages remain capable of reinvention and new relevance. And that will never change.

DYLAN – THE MUSIC:

Where To Begin

BOB DYLAN has released 34 studio albums, 13 live albums, 14 compilations, and beyond the officially released body of work there are an uncountable number of bootlegs. To the newcomer, the massed ranks of his recordings can be intimidating. Where to start? It would be easy to pick up a lesser album and end up putting yourself off Dylan for life. In that spirit, here's a guide to Dylan's essential albums.

1 **The Freewheelin' Bob Dylan**
The best snapshot of early Dylan and the album where his genius began to surface. A potent mix of protest, troubled love songs, and comic 'talkin' blues' numbers.

2-4 **Bringing It All Back Home, Highway 61 Revisited & Blonde On Blonde**
Dylan goes electric in his mid-sixties trilogy. Dylan's revving, rambunctious rock n' roll rips up the rule book. Songs stretch past the then radio-friendly three-minute mark and the lyrics depart for shores never charted before.

5 **The Basement Tapes**
In the wake of his motorbike accident, a less hectic Dylan explores the history of American music and the stranger parts of his imagination

with the help of the Band. The official release is fine but the *A Tree With Roots* bootleg is bigger and better.

6 Blood On The Tracks
The divorce album. Dylan channels his anger and grief into a career-best long-player.

7 Desire
Dylan adopts a gypsy sound to tell a number of tall tales, support a wrongly imprisoned boxer, and, touchingly, to beg his wife to forgive him.

8 Slow Train Coming
Dylan's first Christian album. Smooth-sounding in contrast to the lyrics, which are a raging take on the born-again experience. You can almost see his tongue smoking, his eyes ablaze.

9 Oh Mercy
Dylan redeemed an underwhelming eighties with *Oh Mercy*. Recorded by a man with a worried mind, Dylan's crisis of confidence coincides with a world where (as one song is called) everything is broken.

10 Together Through Life
Dylan's warmest sounding album since *Desire*, although the lyrics continue the trend begun by *Time Out Of Mind*, a sometimes anguished, a sometimes resigned attitude to ageing.

For a more general introduction, you could start with his first volume of *Greatest Hits*, released in

1967, which gives a great taster of the early Dylan. It also is available in practically every library or is inexpensive to buy.

Dylan, when on form, is a superlative live act. During his career he has released a number of live albums. His finest one is *The Bootleg Series Vol. 4 – Bob Dylan Live 1966, The Royal Albert Hall Concert*. Backed by the Hawks/Band and audibly booed by the audience, Dylan rises to his furious best. Includes the infamous 'Judas!' moment.

STUDIO ALBUMS DISCOGRAPHY

Bob Dylan, 1962
The Freewheelin' Bob Dylan, 1963
The Times They Are A-Changin', 1964
Another Side Of Bob Dylan, 1964
Bringing It All Back Home, 1965
Highway 61 Revisited, 1965
Blonde On Blonde, 1966
John Wesley Harding, 1968
Nashville Skyline, 1969
Self Portrait, 1970
New Morning, 1970
Pat Garret And Billy The Kid, 1973
Dylan, 1973
Planet Waves, 1974
Blood On The Tracks, 1975
The Basement Tapes, 1975
Desire, 1976
Street Legal, 1978
Slow Train Coming, 1979
Saved, 1980
Shot Of Love, 1981
Infidels, 1983
Empire Burlesque, 1985
Knocked Out Loaded, 1986
Down In The Groove, 1988
Oh Mercy, 1989
Under The Red Sky, 1990
Good As I Been To You, 1992
World Gone Wrong, 1993
Time Out Of Mind, 1997
Love And Theft, 2001
Modern Times, 2005
Together Through Life, 2009
Christmas In The Heart, 2009

BIBLIOGRAPHY

Barker, Derek (ed.), *Isis – A Bob Dylan Anthology* (Helter Skelter, 2001)

Neil Corcoran (ed.), *Do You Mr Jones? Bob Dylan With The Poets And Professors* (Chatto & Windus, 2002)

Cott, Jonathan (ed.), *Dylan on Dylan* (Hodder & Stoughton, 2006)

Crowe, Cameron, *Biograph* Liner Notes And Text (Special Rider Music, 1985)

Dylan, Bob, *Lyrics 1962-1985* (Grafton, 1993)

Dylan, Bob, *Chronicles: Volume One* (Simon & Schuster, 2004)

Harris, John, (ed.), *Q – Dylan* (IPC Media, 2000)

Heylin, Clinton, A *Life In Stolen Moments – Bob Dylan Day By Day: 1941-1995* (Schirmer Books, 1996)

Heylin, Clinton, *Bob Dylan: The Recording Sessions, 1960-1994* (Macmillan, 1997)

Heylin, Clinton, *Bob Dylan Behind The Shades – Take Two* (Viking, 2000)

Heylin, Clinton, *Revolution In The Air – The Songs Of Bob Dylan Vol. 1: 1957-73* (Constable & Robinson, 2009)

Bob Dylan

Lee, C.P., *Like A Bullet Of Light – The Films Of Bob Dylan* (Helter Skelter, 2000)

MacDonald, Ian, *Revolution In The Head – The Beatles' Records And The Sixties* (Fourth Estate, 1994)

Marcus, Greil, *Invisible Republic – Bob Dylan's Basement Tapes* (Picador, 1995)

Muir, Andrew, *Razor's Edge: Bob Dylan & The Never Ending Tour* (Helter Skelter, 2001)

Scaduto, Anthony, *Bob Dylan* (W.H. Allen & Co, 1971)

Sloman, Larry 'Rastso', *Tell Tale Signs – The Bootleg Series Volume 8* Liner Notes (Sony & BMG Music Entertainment, 2008)

Sounes, Howard, *Down The Highway – The Life Of Bob Dylan* (Black Swan, 2002)

Strong, Martin C., *The Great Rock Discography 7th Edition* (Canongate, 2004)

Williams, Paul, *Watching The River Flow – Observations On His Art-In-Progress 1966-1995* (Omnibus Press, 1996)

Williams, Paul, *Bob Dylan, Performing Artist 1986-1990 & Beyond: Mind Out Of Time* (Omnibus Press, 2004)

Williamson, Nigel, (ed.), *Uncut Legends #1: Dylan* (IPC Media, 2003)